Why Do Investors Act Irrationally?
Behavioral Biases of Herding, Overconfidence, and Overreaction

Ooi Kok Loang
University of Malaya

Series in Business and Finance

VERNON PRESS

www.vernonpress.com

In the Americas:
Vernon Press
1000 N West Street, Suite 1200
Wilmington, Delaware, 19801
United States

In the rest of the world:
Vernon Press
C/Sancti Espiritu 17,
Malaga, 29006
Spain

Series in Business and Finance

Library of Congress Control Number: 2025933287

ISBN: 979-8-8819-0293-3

Also available: 979-8-8819-0242-1 [Hardback]; 979-8-8819-0292-6 [PDF, E-Book]

Cover design by Vernon Press with elements from Freepik.

Table of Contents

List of Figures		v
List of Tables		v
List of Acronyms and Abbreviations		vii
About the Author		ix
Foreword		xi
Preface		xiii
Introduction		xvii
Chapter 1	Why Do Investors Behave Irrationally?	1
Chapter 2	Behavioural Finance: Rethinking Traditional Market Theories	11
Chapter 3	The Power of the Crowd: Decoding Herding Behaviour	29
Chapter 4	Rational or Irrational? The Truth About Herding	45
Chapter 5	The Confidence Trap: Overconfidence in Investing	55
Chapter 6	Overconfidence and Portfolio Mismanagement	65
Chapter 7	The Emotional Rollercoaster: Overreaction and Market Anomalies	73
Chapter 8	Overreaction: The Aftermath of Market News	87

Chapter 9   **The Psychology Behind Biases: What Drives
               Irrationality?**   101

Chapter 10   **Ripple Effects: Consequences of Irrational
               Investor Behaviour**   115

Chapter 11   **Breaking Free From Herding, Overconfidence,
               and Overreaction**   127

Chapter 12   **The Future of Behavioural Finance:
               Technology and Investor Biases**   135

               Conclusion   143

               References   145

               Index   147

List of Figures

Figure 2.1.   Stock Market Performance in selected Asian Countries
(1996-1999)   24
Figure 3.1.   Market Performance During the Dot-Com Bubble (1995-
2002)   35
Figure 8.1.   Market Performance During Initial COVID-19 Outbreak
(Jan-June 2020)   91
Figure 10.1.   GameStop Stock Price Surge During Meme Stock Mania
(Jan-February 2021)   121

List of Tables

Table 2.1.   Key Differences Between Traditional and Behavioural
Finance Theories   17

List of Acronyms and Abbreviations

AAA	Credit Rating (Highest Investment Grade)
ACC	Anterior Cingulate Cortex
AI	Artificial Intelligence
AMC	Asset Management Company
ARKK	ARK Innovation ETF (Cathie Wood's Fund)
BN	Barisan Nasional
CAPM	Capital Asset Pricing Model
CEO	Chief Executive Officer
CIMB	Commerce International Merchant Bankers
COVID	Coronavirus Disease
CRASH	Market Crash
DAX	Deutscher Aktienindex (German Stock Index)
DCA	Dollar Cost Averaging
ECRL	East Coast Rail Link
EMH	Efficient Market Hypothesis
ERM	European Exchange Rate Mechanism
FBM	FTSE Bursa Malaysia Index
FOMO	Fear of Missing Out
FTSE	Financial Times Stock Exchange
GDP	Gross Domestic Product
HSR	High-Speed Rail
IIUM	International Islamic University Malaysia
IMF	International Monetary Fund
KLCI	Kuala Lumpur Composite Index
KPMG	Klynveld Peat Marwick Goerdeler (Big Four Audit Firm)
LTCM	Long-Term Capital Management
MBS	Mortgage-Backed Securities
MPT	Modern Portfolio Theory
NASDAQ	National Association of Securities Dealers Automated Quotations

PH	Pakatan Harapan
PLOS	Public Library of Science (Academic Journal)
QS	Quacquarelli Symonds (University Rankings)
RM	Ringgit Malaysia
UK	United Kingdom
US	United States
VIX	Volatility Index

About the Author

Dr. Ooi Kok Loang is a leading expert in finance, celebrated for his deep insights into behavioural finance and his broad contributions to academia and industry. Currently a faculty member in the Department of Finance at Universiti Malaya, ranked 60th in the 2025 QS World University Rankings, Dr. Ooi previously served as Deputy Dean at City University Malaysia. He holds a Master's and PhD in Finance from Universiti Sains Malaysia (USM) and a Master of Laws from the International Islamic University Malaysia (IIUM), reflecting a rich academic foundation across finance and legal studies.

Dr Ooi's extensive professional background includes advising Malaysia's top 100 listed companies and serving as a board advisor, where he provided strategic insights on finance and corporate governance. His early career as an auditor and business consultant at KPMG, one of the Big Four accounting firms, equipped him with a robust understanding of corporate finance and market strategy. He is a Certified Internal Auditor (CIA) and a Professional Member of the Institute of Internal Auditors, further strengthening his expertise in regulatory and compliance aspects of finance.

Over the past five years, Dr. Ooi has published more than 40 influential papers in high-impact journals, including *Finance Research Letters, Journal of Economic Studies, The Singapore Economic Review, International Journal of Islamic and Middle Eastern Finance and Management,* and *China Finance Review International.* His research delves into behavioural biases like herding, overconfidence, and overreaction, challenging traditional finance theories and reframing investor behaviour through a psychological lens.

A dedicated mentor, Dr. Ooi has successfully guided over 25 PhD students to graduation, fostering the growth of future finance leaders. Central banks and financial institutions, and he regularly shares his expertise on major platforms such as China Talk Show. Dr Ooi's unique combination of academic depth, industry acumen, and regulatory knowledge continues to redefine and elevate the field of behavioural finance, offering critical perspectives on the psychological forces that shape global markets.

Foreword

Human beings have long held that financial markets are efficient, data-driven systems that make rational decisions. But history reminds us that economic booms, busts and disasters usually spring from irrational behavior, distorted thinking and emotional involvement. The book is about behavioral finance and what it teaches us about the biases that drive both market movement and investment decisions. The book is heavily downloaded from the expertise of Dr. Ooi Kok Loang from Universiti Malaya.

Although technological advancements have altered the financial landscape, they have failed to eliminate unjustified behavior. Why? However, the advent of algorithmic trading, AI-led financial models and the proliferation of DeFi systems has made this process increasingly complex. These advancements not only expedite processes and make products more readily available, but they also enable individuals to engage in more systematic risk-taking activities, including speculation and market manipulation. The behavioral biases that affect the most established banks can also have repercussions. The use of AI in trading and investing can raise concerns about the potential impact of artificial intelligence on market efficiency as a result of making random algorithms based on historical data.

This book seeks to bring together the fields of banking and psychology by analyzing past financial crises and incorporating what is known about recent technological breakthroughs. It delves deep into the topic of how irrational behavior still impacts financial markets, even with all the tech that's out there. To top it all off, it helps politicians, investors, and financial experts navigate the ever-changing and uncertain financial world by outlining a framework for identifying and reducing these risks.

Prof. Dr. Sevenpri Candra
Binus University, Indonesia

Preface

Finance is often portrayed as a world of cool-headed calculations governed by spreadsheets, projections, and rational assessments of risks and rewards. But in truth, behind every market movement and every investment decision lies something far more dynamic and unpredictable: human psychology. No matter how sophisticated our models or advanced our algorithms are, the reality is that finance is a deeply human endeavour. This bookpeels back the layers of traditional finance and reveal the forces that truly drive market behaviour—the biases, fears, hopes, and instincts that make us human.

In "Chapter 1: Why Do Investors Behave Irrationally?" we start with a question that goes to the heart of behavioural finance. If markets are supposed to be rational and investors are expected to act in their own best interests, why, then, do we see such wild swings in sentiment? Why do investors repeatedly make decisions that, in hindsight, seem reckless or irrational? This opening chapter delves into the psychology of investing, exploring how our brains are wired for emotional responses that once served us well in survival but can betray us in the world of financial markets. Here, we uncover concepts like loss aversion, where the fear of losing overshadows the excitement of gaining, and bounded rationality, which shows that even the best intentions are limited by our cognitive biases and emotional inclinations.

"Chapter 2: Behavioural Finance: Rethinking Traditional Market Theories" challenges the bedrock assumptions that have long dominated finance. Traditional theories, such as the Efficient Market Hypothesis, hold that markets are rational and that prices always reflect all available information (Fama, 1970). Behavioural finance, however, argues otherwise, suggesting that emotions, cognitive biases, and psychological pressures often cause deviations from rationality. In this chapter, we explore how the field of behavioural finance emerged as a response to the limitations of classical theories, providing us with a more nuanced view of the market. It invites readers to reconsider the assumption that markets are perfectly efficient and introduces the idea that the human element, with all its imperfections, plays a critical role in shaping market dynamics.

In "Chapter 3: The Power of the Crowd: Decoding Herding Behaviour," we enter the complex and often perplexing world of herding behaviour. This chapter examines the human tendency to follow the crowd, especially when uncertainty looms. Drawing from historical examples, from the tulip mania of the seventeenth century to the tech boom of the late 1990s, we uncover the social and psychological underpinnings of herding. We look at how the actions of others can act as a powerful signal, driving individuals to abandon their own judgements and follow the masses. Herding is one of the most powerful forces in finance, and this chapter sheds light on why it is so compelling—and often so destructive.

Following closely is "Chapter 4: Rational or Irrational? The Truth About Herding," which explores the fine line between rational and irrational herding. Here, we dissect information-based herding—where people follow the crowd because they believe others have valuable information—and reputational herding, where individuals follow the majority to avoid the social or professional risks of going against the grain. The chapter forces us to confront an uncomfortable truth: not all herding is irrational. Sometimes, the crowd does know best. However, distinguishing rational from irrational herding is no easy feat, and this chapter examines the consequences of getting it wrong.

The trap of overconfidence takes centre stage in "Chapter 5: The Confidence Trap: Overconfidence in Investing." Overconfidence is one of the most pervasive and subtle biases in finance, and it affects novices and experts alike. Investors often believe they are smarter, better informed, or more skilled than they actually are, which leads to risky behaviour and poor decisions. This chapter unpacks the origins of overconfidence, showing how a few successful trades can create a false sense of mastery. We examine the illusion of knowledge, where investors mistakenly equate information with understanding and explore how this inflated confidence can blind investors to real risks.

Building on this theme, "Chapter 6: Overconfidence and Portfolio Mismanagement" delves into the practical consequences of overconfidence in the world of portfolio management. Overconfident investors are more likely to trade excessively, ignore diversification, and take on excessive risk, believing they have the skill to time the market or pick the next winning stock. This chapter provides a sobering look at how overconfidence can lead to portfolio mismanagement, exposing investors to unnecessary losses and volatility. Through real-world case studies and research, we learn why humility and caution are essential for long-term success in investing.

In "Chapter 7: The Emotional Rollercoaster: Overreaction and Market Anomalies," we explore the emotional highs and lows that define investor behaviour. This chapter takes us through the phenomena of overreaction—both euphoric buying and panic-driven selling—showing how markets swing from one extreme to another based on the emotions of their participants. Overreaction is the engine behind many market anomalies, such as the January Effect and the Weekend Effect, where prices deviate from expected patterns due to collective psychological behaviour rather than rational analysis. This chapter highlights how emotion, more than any financial model, often dictates market direction.

Continuing with the theme of emotion-driven decision-making, "Chapter 8: Overreaction: The Aftermath of Market News" examines how investors respond to sudden news and events. Whether it is a disappointing earnings report, a geopolitical crisis, or a natural disaster, news events trigger emotional responses that can lead to overreaction and extreme price movements. This chapter brings to life the ways in which fear and greed drive investors to overreact to market news, often exacerbating the very problems they fear. From the 2008 financial meltdown to the COVID-19 pandemic, we see how markets are profoundly shaped by collective overreaction, underscoring the impact of psychological dynamics in times of crisis.

In "Chapter 9: The Psychology Behind Biases: What Drives Irrationality?," we journey deeper into the brain itself, exploring the neuroscience behind investor behaviour. This chapter introduces us to key brain structures—the amygdala, striatum, and prefrontal cortex—and examines how each plays a role in our financial decision-making. We look at how the amygdala, the brain's centre for emotion, can trigger fear responses that lead to panic selling and how the striatum, with its craving for rewards, can fuel overconfidence and risk-taking. This exploration of the mind reveals that our biases are not just bad habits—they are the product of deeply ingrained neural pathways that shape our reactions to risk, uncertainty, and reward.

"Chapter 10: Ripple Effects: Consequences of Irrational Investor Behaviour" takes a broader view, examining how individual biases can lead to market-wide consequences. Through events like the dot-com bubble, the 2008 financial crisis, and the GameStop saga of 2021, we see how irrational behaviour by individuals can ripple through the market, causing bubbles, crashes, and crises that impact entire economies. This chapter demonstrates that investor psychology is not just a personal issue—it has real, tangible effects on the world, affecting jobs, businesses, and livelihoods. The chapter serves as a powerful reminder of the collective impact of individual decisions and the importance of understanding and managing irrational behaviour.

But it is not all cautionary tales. In "Chapter 11: Breaking Free from Herding, Overconfidence, and Overreaction," we explore strategies for overcoming these biases. Drawing on research in behavioural economics and psychology, we introduce tools such as behavioural nudges, mindfulness practices, and rule-based investing to help readers make better financial decisions. This chapter is about reclaiming control, learning to recognize when biases are at play, and adopting strategies that counteract our natural tendencies. It is an empowering chapter, offering practical insights for those who want to approach investing with a more disciplined, rational mindset.

Finally, we conclude with "Chapter 12: The Future of Behavioural Finance: Technology and Investor Biases." The financial landscape is changing rapidly, with artificial intelligence, big data, and machine learning transforming how we invest. But these technologies also present new challenges. Will AI make us more rational, or will it amplify our biases in new ways? This chapter explores the intersection of human psychology and technology, considering the role of robo-advisors, behavioural algorithms, and the digital tools that promise to shape the future of finance. As we move into an era where technology plays a more dominant role in decision-making, this chapter challenges readers to consider what it means to remain human in an increasingly automated world.

Introduction

If you believe that finance is all about numbers and calculations, think again. Every stock ticker, trading floor, and portfolio tells us about ourselves, about human nature, why we make the decisions we do, and how those decisions influence the world around us. This book encourages you to discover that tale, to enter the secret side of the market, where psychology, emotion, and behaviour intersect to form the rhythms of financial life. This book delves into a world in which stocks and shares are more than just assets; they represent our most fundamental inclinations, goals, anxieties, and, occasionally, folly. In the following sections, you will learn how understanding these instincts may not only help you become a better investor but also provide a fresh perspective on financial markets—one in which people, not just statistics, determine the economic results.

Why do some individuals follow every market trend only to get caught in a tsunami of loss? Why can a quick increase in a stock's price make even the most conservative investors feel as if they are losing money? Why, despite all we know, do we keep making the same mistakes? The answers to these issues are not just contained in financial theories; they are also ingrained in our brains, prejudices, and the enormous influences that impact how we think, feel and behave towards money (Richards, 2024).

This voyage starts with a look at herding, the tendency that pushes us to follow the crowd, even when we know the precipice is directly ahead. Herding is a strong force that causes booms and crashes, and it may persuade even the most reasonable investors to disregard warning signs in search of the "next big thing." Next, we will look at overconfidence, the attractive but hazardous assumption that we are wiser than everyone else and have discovered a pattern that no one else has. Overconfidence is a gambler's buddy and an investor's enemy, and it is one of the most frequent ways individuals get into financial trouble.

We will look more closely at this overreaction. This bias transforms us into emotional traders, reacting to every story, dips, and spikes with actions that seldom support our long-term objectives. In an era of rapid knowledge, overreaction is rampant, fuelled by media cycles that demand attention and social feeds that amp up every market rumour.

However, understanding these patterns is just beginning. This book is about mastering the influences that affect our financial behaviour, not just recognising them. Imagine being able to recognise when you are following the herd and having the fortitude to steer your route instead. Consider developing a solid investing philosophy that will keep you focused, even when the market is noisy. Imagine making choices based on clarity and conviction rather than response or regret. This is what behavioural finance may provide: the ability to understand oneself as well as the market.

Then, there is the future—a thrilling, uncertain environment created by AI, social media, and digital platforms that have made investment more accessible and volatile than ever before. Technology is revolutionising finance at an unprecedented pace, providing us with the ability to analyse data and make choices quicker than any investor in history. However, this power also creates a new set of hazards. Artificial intelligence may provide insights, but it may also accentuate human prejudice. Social media may help us learn, but it can also create digital echo chambers in which excitement, fear, and frenzy reinforce each other. In this book, we will delve deeply into these technological advancements, learning how to utilise these tools without allowing them to exploit us.

A growing amount of research in contemporary behavioural finance links human biases and technological advancements, especially in light of the explosive growth of social media, 5G technology, and artificial intelligence, which are having previously unheard-of effects on investors' decision-making processes. Investors can now process enormous volumes of data and make judgements in a fraction of the time, thanks to the development of artificial intelligence. But even though AI has previously unheard-of benefits, it also exacerbates innate human prejudices. AI recommendation systems, for instance, might provide recommendations for particular investment possibilities based on user preferences and historical behaviour. This could inadvertently reinforce biases like herd mentality or overconfidence, which would ultimately impact market efficiency and fairness.

In a similar vein, social media's power has significantly increased, enabling investors to quickly learn about and engage in conversations. Nevertheless, this has given rise to new problems—the "digital echo chamber effect" on social media platforms frequently puts investors in unduly positive states as updates and tweets keep escalating feelings. In situations like the Bitcoin bubble, where social media was crucial to the flow of information, this emotional escalation helps to promote collectively irrational behaviour.

These technical phenomena are not limited to the IT industry; they also have an impact on ethical concerns around behavioural nudging. Governments and financial organisations have implemented behavioural interventions extensively since Thaler and Sunstein's "nudge" hypothesis was first presented. These interventions use "gentle" nudges to influence people's decisions. However, this notion has been criticised, especially in relation to the violation of individual autonomy. Critics contend that when interventions rely too heavily on models of human behaviour, nudging may subtly violate people's autonomy and free will, making it potentially opaque and even coercive.

Furthermore, behavioural economics' reputation has suffered as a result of the recent Harvard data fraud controversy. The controversy raised questions about whether the experimental findings that behavioural economics depends on actually reflect market behaviour and revealed unethical practices in academic data gathering and processing. Widespread debates concerning the rigour of empirical studies and the transparency of research methodologies in behavioural finance were spurred by this episode. Both in academia and the general public, it resulted in a major decline in trust in both domains.

As technology develops further, behavioural finance will encounter both new possibilities and difficulties. Technology has made the market environment more complex, whether it is through the use of artificial intelligence or the impact of social media. This book's subsequent chapters will explore how these technologies are influencing investor psychology and behaviour, both by providing new chances to reduce conventional behavioural biases and by making it simpler for investors to be bound by them. Investors will be more equipped to handle the shifting financial markets if they are aware of these recent technical developments.

Understanding the many theoretical frameworks that influence how we interpret market behaviour is essential to the study of financial markets. It's crucial to define the phrase "classical" or "traditional" views of economics, even though many people may use it. The term "classical" is frequently linked to specific schools of thought in the economic literature. The first is the standard economic theory known as "Marginalist Theory," which emphasises elements like endowments, consumer preferences, and production methods and holds that markets move towards full employment. Walras, Wicksell, Menger, Marshall, and Pigou are important figures in this lineage, and this framework is still being developed by contemporary contributors like Blanchard, Stiglitz, and Summers. A more demand-driven strategy based on the examination of physical production and distribution characteristics is provided by the second school, Classical-Keynesian Theory. Smith, Ricardo, Marx, and Sraffa's writings are the most well-known examples of this tradition, with more recent versions referencing Keynes' 1936 General Theory. Since the term "classical" has been used widely throughout history, it is crucial to make clear if it refers to the Marginalist Theory in the context of this work.

Furthermore, behavioural finance is more in line with post-Keynesian and Sraffian traditions, especially in its acknowledgement of path dependency and its criticism of the presumptions of market efficiency and rationality, despite frequently being framed as a challenge to conventional economic theories

(Lavoie, 2014). The limitations of marginalist assumptions have been highlighted by individuals such as Sraffa (1961), who demonstrated that the simplistic models of equilibrium that predominate in the marginalist perspective are insufficient to explain the intricacies of real-world economics. In this sense, behavioural finance offers a deeper comprehension of the social and psychological factors influencing market dynamics, recognising that investor behaviour is impacted by both innate human bias and irrationality as well as quantitative models. It will be crucial to understand as we move through this book that behavioural finance incorporates ideas from these alternative traditions, providing a more thorough understanding of market forces that take into consideration human emotion as well as cognitive constraints that are overlooked by traditional theories.

This is not simply a book for finance experts or market insiders; it is for anybody interested in understanding the market dynamics and psychology that define our financial life. Whether you are a seasoned investor or just starting in the world of finance, you will discover tools, insights, and tactics to help you think better, act more autonomously, and invest with a purpose that matches who you are.

So, if you are ready to understand the market's hidden forces, see past the statistics, and take charge of your financial destiny in an educated and empowered manner, this book was intended for you. Welcome to the adventure of better knowing the market and yourself than ever before.

Chapter 1

Why Do Investors Behave Irrationally?

Imagine entering a thriving financial market—a vast stage where fortunes are made and broken, and individuals pursue fantasies of independence, stability, and prestige. Everyone wants to outwit the system, overcome obstacles, and bask in the warmth of accomplishment. The idea of a calm and calculating investor who is laser-focused, level-headed, and endlessly reasonable often dominates the public imagination. But this picture is a mirage, a soothing story that fails to capture the human aspect of investment. The fact is that all investors, regardless of experience or knowledge, are prone to making illogical judgements influenced by emotions, biases, and psychological traps. This chapter is about peeling back the layers of human behaviour to understand why, despite our best intentions, humans continue to behave in ways that defy rationality.

Consider this: Michael is at a backyard cookout, surrounded by pals who cannot stop gushing about the newest electric car manufacturer. They have all invested, and the talk is brimming with anticipation. "I have doubled my money in just three months!" his friend Brian exclaims, a drink in hand, his face beaming with pride. Michael, feeling the heat of everyone's excitement, decides to attend the party. After all, he does not want to be the only one left out. He takes out his phone right there, disregarding the smoky smell of the grill and the children playing in the garden, and buys stock in the firm without hesitation. The stock continues to rise, and Michael feels like a genius. He believes, "This is it! The ride to easy wealth!" But what Michael does not see is that he is gambling, caught up in the crowd mentality. Fast forward a few weeks: the firm fails to meet a critical production goal, and the price plunges overnight. The exhilaration fades, replaced with a pit in his gut. Michael watches helplessly as the value plummets, hoping he can rewind time. What seemed to be an easy victory becomes a brutal lesson in pursuing the crowd.

Then there is Emily, an experienced investor who believes herself a market expert. She is the sort of person who reads financial periodicals obsessively, her coffee going cold as she sifts through earnings reports and market analysis. Emily has made a few good decisions in the past, and she begins to believe she has a sixth instinct for these things. When she learns about a potential biotech business, she thinks it will revolutionise cancer treatment. Ignoring the tiny voice in her brain warning her about the dangers of the biotech industry, she gambles big. She believes she is wiser than the ordinary investor and has insights that others do not. However, the market does not care about her confidence. A few months later, the business experiences unanticipated regulatory setbacks, and the once-soaring stock plummets. Emily's "sure thing" develops into a nightmare. Overconfidence drove her to disregard warning signals and risk everything on a hunch. As she sits gazing at her depleting account balance, she realises she is not as indestructible as she imagined. The market has a way of bringing even the most confident players down.

And then there is Dave, who is always cautious and plays things safe. Dave has been investing in index funds for years, gradually but steadily increasing his fortune. But one evening, while browsing through his phone, he stumbles across a breaking news alert: "MARKET CRASH IMMINENT!" The large letters seem to yell at him, causing a rush of dread. The article warns of an economic disaster, and Dave feels the same terror he had in 2008 when he witnessed his parents' funds go. Panic set in. Without hesitation, Dave connects to his broking account and sells everything. He sighs a sigh of relief, believing he has averted calamity. But days and weeks pass, and the market does not fall; instead, it slowly grows, hitting new highs. Dave watches helplessly as the value of his previous assets increases beyond where he sold them. He realises he was behaving out of fear, responding to sensationalist news. He was not defending himself; he was allowing fear to determine his financial destiny. Now, the consequence of his overreaction is more than lost earnings; it is a deep sadness that he did not believe his approach.

These are the tales of investors at their most human: Michael, caught up in the excitement of the crowd; Emily, overconfident in her talents; and Dave, paralysed by dread. Each felt they were making the correct move and operating logically, yet each succumbed to the same pressures that often derail investors. The attraction of easy money, the confidence in one's invincibility, and the terror that comes with uncertainty—all of these emotions combine to form a perfect storm, clouding judgement and leading even the most intelligent individuals to make dumb decisions. It serves as a reminder that investing is about more than simply conquering the markets; it is also about mastering one's illogical conduct.

Battle Between Traditional Finance and Behavioural Finance

The classic financial concept of the rational investor has long served as the foundation of economic theory. The Efficient Market Hypothesis, which has dominated the area of finance for decades, holds that markets are efficient because investors behave rationally, analyse information correctly, and make choices that maximise profits. However, history clearly shows that the truth is very different. Investors are emotional and prone to cognitive shortcuts, social pressure, and impulsive reactions that may result in overvaluations, collapses, and financial catastrophes (Baker et al., 2019). The stock market is more than simply a collection of facts; it is a psychological warfare in which emotions such as fear and greed are as potent as any economic indicator.

Consider the 2008 housing market collapse, which started with the promise of prosperity and the expectation that property prices would continue to grow indefinitely. This disaster was fuelled by massively unreasonable behaviour. Investors, homeowners, and financial institutions flocked into the housing market, all motivated by overconfidence and a collective refusal to accept the hazards. Banks made loans to individuals who could not afford them, hoping that increasing housing values would offset the risks. Overconfident homeowners, confident that they could continue refinancing their mortgages, borrowed more than they could afford. Investors purchased mortgage-backed securities they did not comprehend, optimistic that the market would never fall. This was not logical decision-making; it was a communal illusion based on optimism, greed, and denial—a stark reminder that irrationality can transform whole economies.

Herding Among Investors

Herding is another central element of investor irrationality, with origins in human evolutionary history. Consider early people on the savannas, confronted with the unexpected relocation of their group. If everyone else began fleeing, it was typically a good idea to join them—safety in numbers was frequently synonymous with survival. This tendency is still with us now, and it manifests itself powerfully in the financial markets. When investors see others investing in a particular asset—whether it is a rising tech company, a hot cryptocurrency, or a freshly touted commodity—they feel compelled to join in. The fear of missing out, or FOMO, takes hold, compelling investors to act before fully grasping the underlying value. They do not want to be left behind, while others seem to earn quickly.

Consider the situation of Bitcoin. Imagine it is late 2017, and everyone you know is talking about Bitcoin. The air is charged with reports of individuals earning millions overnight, and headlines shout about the new digital gold rush. Your barber tells you he is made 400% on his investment. Your relative, who typically cannot stop talking about sports, is now an authority in cryptocurrency. The rush seems almost mystical, as if you are seeing the beginning of a financial revolution. People are coming in to purchase Bitcoin not because they understand blockchain technology or believe in its long-term potential but because everyone else is. The rationale seems flawless: if so many others are becoming wealthy, why not you?

The media fosters the craze, flooding every platform with tales of early adopters who are suddenly billionaires sitting on boats. You can practically hear the clock ticking. This is your one chance to earn more money than you have ever dreamt of, and if you do not move now, it will slide through your fingers. So you purchase. Perhaps you are buying a lot. And for a time, it feels fantastic. The value skyrockets, and each passing day reinforces that you have made the correct choice. But, almost as quickly as it surged, Bitcoin began to sink. The numbers on your app are no longer green; they are crimson. People start selling in a frenzy, and before you realise it, the enchantment has gone. All those visions of easy fortune fade as quickly as they came. This is the force of herding—when individuals are motivated not by their knowledge but by the soothing idea that if everyone else is doing it, it must be correct. It is not investing; it is following the mob off a cliff, fuelled by the shared conviction that prices will continue to rise indefinitely. It is exciting until it is not.

Herding behaviour is not new. In reality, it dates back to the seventeenth century, during the notorious tulip frenzy in the Netherlands. Consider this: tulips are the latest trend. Yes, tulips—those lovely, vibrant flowers that blossom in spring. They were a symbol of riches and importance, and everyone desired one. Prices rose dramatically in response to increasing demand. People from all walks of life, from farmers to noblemen, were purchasing and selling tulip bulbs, hoping to make a profit. The excitement became so extreme that, at one time, a single tulip bulb might cost more than a competent worker's entire wage. It was ridiculous, but at the time, it seemed entirely sensible. The premise was simple: if people were prepared to spend so much, the price had to be reasonable. Crucially, they believed the price would continue to rise. The concept that a flower might be worth a lot seems to make sense until it does not. The boom burst, prices fell nearly immediately, and many individuals lost everything. It was not about the tulips; it was about the collective psyche of people who were engrossed in a story that obscured reality. It is a classic case of herding, motivated by the human impulse to seek safety in numbers, even if those numbers are heading towards calamity.

Overconfidence

Overconfidence, on the other hand, functions at the individual level. Imagine Jake. Jake is the person at the party who has an opinion on everything—stocks, sports, politics, you name it. He is unquestionably brilliant, and he has made a few profitable bets in the past. Jake's victories have given him a feeling of invincibility, a conviction that he can see things that others cannot. When Jake learns about a hot new biotech business working on novel cancer therapy, he decides to go all in. The more he reads, the more confident he grows. He does not see the dangers; he sees himself making a brilliant move that will demonstrate, once again, that he is ahead of the curve. He rejects his friends' cautionary advice, dismisses the concept of diversifying his assets, and invests all of his resources in this single stock. For a time, it seems he is correct. The price rises, and Jake feels like a genius. He is confident he is on his way to unbelievable fortune.

However, biotechnology is dangerous. A few months later, the firm is experiencing setbacks—clinical studies are not progressing as expected, and regulators are concerned—the stock plummets. Jake's portfolio is now worth a fraction of its previous value. His once-soaring confidence comes crashing down. Jake did not view the business objectively; he saw what he wanted to see—a mirror of his own supposed greatness. Overconfidence is like a fog that obscures judgement. It makes individuals feel they are unique and capable of predicting the unexpected. It causes people to lose sight of the fact that the market is essentially unpredictable, and no one, no matter how brilliant, is immune to it.

The dot-com boom of the late 1990s is one of the most spectacular instances of collective overconfidence. The internet was changing everything, and everyone wanted a piece of the future. Investors, large and small, poured money into tech businesses that needed more earnings, a clear business plan, and occasionally no product. But it did not matter. The story was so compelling: "The internet is the future, and if you invest now, you will be rich beyond your wildest dreams." People thought they were part of a revolution, and that conviction closed their eyes to fundamental economic concepts. They did not care if the firms did not have any income or if their business strategies were scribbled on the back of napkins. They believed that the internet would alter everything, and they wanted to be a part of it. The excitement drove the market to an unsustainable frenzy. However, it is important to note that only a small portion of the population participated in the bubble. Despite the widespread media hype and the belief that everyone was involved, the reality was that many investors either remained cautious or missed out on the speculative surge entirely. Stocks that should have been worthless were worth millions due to speculation and overconfidence. When reality struck, the bubble popped, and billions of dollars went almost immediately. It was a harsh warning that confidence without substance may lead to disaster.

Overconfidence also influences daily investing choices. Famous research by Barber and Odean (2000) discovered that individual investors who traded regularly underperformed the market owing to overconfidence. These investors felt they had better insights or could time the market well, so they traded excessively and paid hefty transaction fees. Ironically, their attempts to "beat the market" sometimes resulted in worse returns than a conventional buy-and-hold approach. Overconfidence produces the illusion of control—the perception that we have more control over outcomes than we do. It leads to judgements that disregard crucial investment concepts like diversification and risk control.

While overconfidence encourages investors to engage in irresponsible behaviour, overreaction is another psychological bias that often leads to illogical actions. Humans are hardwired to respond quickly to new information—an evolutionary characteristic that helped our ancestors survive. However, in the financial markets, this might lead to impulsive responses that are not necessarily consistent with logical decision-making. Investors often overreact to both positive and negative news. A firm misses its profit projections by a slight margin, and the market reacts with a sell-off that wipes off billions of dollars in market value despite the fact that the long-term fundamentals are unaffected. On the other hand, a cheerful piece of news might cause a boom in purchasing, with investors bidding up the price well above what is warranted by the actual improvement.

Tesla's situation illustrates the phenomena of overreaction. Tesla's stock has been very volatile in recent years, mainly owing to overreactions to both good and bad news. Elon Musk's tweets, manufacturing milestones, and news about regulatory hurdles often cause substantial price changes. Investors, fuelled by emotion, rush to purchase or sell, exacerbating stock price fluctuations. This volatility is usually driven by the emotional reactions of investors attempting to capitalise on—or flee from—the day's news rather than the underlying company fundamentals. Overreaction presents chances for individuals who can keep their emotions under control, but for most investors, the impulse to "do something" in response to news often leads to irrational actions.

To really understand why investors act irrationally, we must go beyond individual biases and include the impact of emotions and social dynamics. Investing is a very emotional experience. It is about hopes, dreams, concerns, and anxieties. The fear of losing money is a strong motivation, and it may lead to panic selling during market downturns. The agony of loss often surpasses the delight of gain, a phenomenon known as loss aversion. Investors sometimes cling to losing holdings for too long, afraid to accept a loss since it seems like admitting defeat. Instead, they expect that the market will recover, even when the data shows otherwise. This emotional commitment to assets may result in considerable underperformance because investors rely on hope rather than making sensible choices based on fresh knowledge.

Fear and Greed

Fear and greed are the two emotions that underpin most of the irrational behaviour in financial markets. Greed drives investors to seek profits and buy into rising markets without examining if the values are reasonable. It convinces them that they can get wealthy rapidly and that the chance is too excellent to pass up. Fear, on the other hand, causes panic and rash judgements. When markets tumble, the inclination is to sell and get out before things worsen. This cycle of fear and greed causes volatility as investors fluctuate between joy and terror. Understanding these emotional motivations is critical to making sound investing choices. It requires discipline, self-awareness, and a willingness to face our unreasonable behaviour.

The social side of investing adds an extra degree of difficulty. Humans are social creatures who are impacted by the behaviours and attitudes of others around them. In financial markets, this is known as herd behaviour. When everyone else is purchasing, it seems riskier not to buy. When everyone else is selling, it looks dangerous to hold out. This herd mentality has the potential to create bubbles as prices are propelled higher and higher by the collective actions of investors who are all following the same crowd. The Bitcoin mania of recent years is an excellent illustration of this. Bitcoin's meteoric growth was fuelled in large part by social media, reports of individuals making millions, and the notion that this was a once-in-a-lifetime chance. Investors bought into the hoopla not because they understood the technology or saw its long-term potential but because everyone else was doing it. When the boom burst, many people suffered enormous financial losses.

Even expert investors are susceptible to irrational behaviour. The 2008 financial crisis served as a vivid reminder that even the brightest individuals, equipped with complex models and massive quantities of data, may make disastrous judgements. Overconfidence, herding, and the notion that "this time is different" resulted in hazardous lending practices, complicated financial instruments, and an unsustainable housing boom. The crisis demonstrated that irrational behaviour is not limited to individual investors; it can infect whole institutions and impact the economy as a whole. Successful and unsuccessful investors often vary in their abilities to recognise these biases and take actions to limit their effects. It is not about eliminating biases—that is practically impossible—but about acknowledging them and having the discipline to adhere to a well-stated plan.

It is crucial to incorporate past market occurrences that clearly demonstrate the dynamics of human behaviour influencing financial decisions in order to gain a deeper knowledge of irrational behaviour in investing. An excellent example of overconfidence and herd mentality in action is the Dotcom Bubble of the late 1990s. Investors poured money into tech businesses that had no profitable business strategies because they believed in the internet's alluring promise. Fear of missing out (FOMO) and unrelenting optimism created unsustainable prices, and when reality set in, the market crashed, and huge amounts of money were lost. This is a powerful illustration of how irrational enthusiasm and herd mentality can skew market prices and cause catastrophic disasters. The global financial crisis of 2008 is another notable example of how overconfidence in the property market, supported by faulty risk assessments and unrestrained lending, led to a bubble that eventually burst and caused a downturn in the economy that impacted millions of people.

A crucial component of behavioural finance, loss aversion, also needs more explanation in order to link theory to practical investing. The psychological phenomenon known as loss aversion occurs when the joy of a comparable gain is less powerful than the anguish of a loss. When it comes to investing, this bias can cause people to sell valuable assets quickly in order to lock in gains while holding onto failing investments for an excessive amount of time in the hopes of a recovery. Many investors, for instance, held onto depreciating assets in the belief that prices would eventually return to their earlier highs during the 2008 financial crisis, despite the fact that doing so frequently resulted in missed recovery opportunities.

Furthermore, the notion that investors are "supposed to be rational" is more complicated than it first appears. The Efficient Market Hypothesis (EMH) and other traditional finance theories have long maintained that investors behave rationally and that markets reflect all available information. But even this assumption is coming under more and more scrutiny. Behavioural finance questions the idea of the "rational investor," arguing that people may interpret rationality differently depending on their social context, emotions, and biases. For example, during market booms, what could seem like logical choices based on a positive perspective can easily turn into a herd mentality motivated by the need for rapid gains and societal pressures. A new perspective on market dynamics and investor behaviour is made possible by acknowledging that human decision-making is influenced by psychological elements in addition to the icy logic of statistics.

The 1998 collapse of Long-Term Capital Management (LTCM), a hedge fund, is one of the most well-known case studies that highlights the psychological biases and irrational behaviour in investing. Two economics Nobel laureates, Myron Scholes and Robert Merton, were among the group of financial specialists who formed LTCM. They were quite confident in their capacity to forecast and control financial markets. In order to wager on interest rate convergence and market stability, the fund's strategy made use of complex models and significant leverage. On paper, their approach made sense because it was based on mathematical models that reduced risk and assumed market efficiency.

But the fund's herd mentality and overconfidence in its algorithms caused it to overlook the possibility of catastrophic market shocks, which ultimately proved devastating. A worldwide financial crisis was brought on by Russia's 1998 debt default, which resulted in significant losses for LTCM's highly leveraged assets. The managers of LTCM were overpowered by the very dangers they had considered insignificant, and the fund's model had not taken into consideration the likelihood of such an occurrence, even with its knowledgeable staff. A clear reminder of the perils of overconfidence and the limitations of depending exclusively on intricate financial models is provided by the demise of LTCM. The failure of LTCM demonstrates how even the most intelligent brains can be prone to cognitive biases, missing the very human element of uncertainty, emotions, and social influences that drive the market, much like the dot-com boom or the housing crisis of 2008. This scenario also emphasises the value of comprehending market psychology and the need to develop methods that take human behaviour into consideration rather than solely depending on statistical models, which may not work in the most dire circumstances.

The process of being a sensible investor starts with self-awareness. It is about identifying the emotions, biases, and societal influences that impact our judgements and devising tactics to combat them. It is essential to recognise that investing is more than simply a numbers game; it is also a psychological one. The market is a complicated system shaped by the aggregate activities of people, each with their aspirations, fears, and prejudices. Understanding why we behave irrationally allows us to begin to make better decisions—decisions based on logical thinking rather than emotion or the behaviours of the herd.

Chapter 2

Behavioural Finance: Rethinking Traditional Market Theories

Consider a universe in which everyone is totally logical, and emotions such as fear, greed, and enthusiasm have no part in decision-making. This is the basis on which conventional finance is constructed. It implies that investors are like computers, devoid of emotion, digesting massive quantities of data with accuracy and always making the right decision. Traditional theories claim that markets are efficient, that prices always represent the fundamental worth of assets, and that it is only possible to constantly beat the market by taking on more risk. For a long time, this was the accepted fact, a soothing fiction we told ourselves about how the financial world operated.

However, the actual world is chaotic, unexpected, and full of emotion. Logical calculators do not populate the actual world but humans, complete with defects, oddities, and prejudices. If markets were actually efficient, how would we explain the booms, collapses, and irrational exuberance that have changed the financial landscape throughout time? How can we explain the panics that cause markets to plummet, the bubbles that expand beyond any fair value, and the investors who pour money into firms with no incomes, profits, or prospects? To properly understand financial markets, we must delve beyond the tidy mathematics and efficient market models and investigate the human psychology that underpins it all. Here is where behavioural finance comes in.

Basic of Behavioural Finance

Behavioural finance arose as a reaction to the shortcomings of conventional finance. It is a discipline that combines economics and psychology, questioning long-held assumptions that investors are always rational and markets are always efficient. It acknowledges the intricacies of human nature—the emotions, prejudices, and cognitive limitations that often lead us wrong. Behavioural finance acknowledges that investors are not cold, calculating robots; they are humans with the same fears, hopes, and blunders as everyone else. The tale of behavioural finance is the story of human behaviour, and it starts by addressing long-held economic beliefs.

Consider a market that runs like clockwork. In a world where every new piece of information is immediately absorbed, prices are always correct, and investors make judgements with the calm precision of a chess genius plotting their next move. Traditional finance envisions a logical, efficient market in which every dollar goes to its proper location and every risk is evaluated. This universe has no irrational fears or late-night urges, simply logic, calculation, and efficiency. It is a nice and tidy society, with individuals making decisions to maximise their profits while minimising their dangers. For decades, economists believed in this financial universe—until actual life told them otherwise.

The EMH is a significant theory that has long served as the foundation for this rational market paradigm. Eugene Fama developed EMH in the 1960s, which holds that stock prices reflect all available information quickly and precisely. The idea holds that every investor is rational and that their collective judgements result in prices that consistently represent the actual worth of things. Imagine attending an auction, but instead of competitive bids, you have a room full of individuals who know precisely how much an item is worth. In this case, there is no guessing or emotion—only complete information. According to the EMH, attempting to beat the market is useless since all essential information is already baked into each stock's price. It is like trying to run a race in which everyone begins at the same time and on the same footing—no one can continuously lead.

Efficient Market Hypothesis

The EMH, which maintains that markets are efficient and always represent all available information, has long been a pillar of conventional financial theory. This perspective, however, oversimplifies how complicated financial markets are. Without taking into account the subtle differences within the theory itself, EMH is frequently presented in a binary framework—markets are either efficient, or they are not. Three categories of market efficiency—weak, semi-strong, and strong—that recognise varying degrees of market pricing efficiency were first proposed by Eugene Fama in his 1970 paper. Even the EMH's proponents acknowledge that markets can display inefficiencies in specific situations, such as at times of high speculation or market bubbles, even though it suggests that investors cannot regularly outperform the market through stock selection or market timing. Two notable instances of investor behaviour deviating from rationality and resulting in asset mispricing are the dot-com bubble of the 1990s and the 2008 financial crisis. Although the EMH explains why it is difficult for experts to regularly "beat the market," it is unable to explain the psychological aspects affecting market movements or the irrational exuberance that fuels bubbles.

Traditional finance theories have progressively incorporated behavioural insights throughout time, departing from the rigorous rationality that early models presumed. As behavioural finance research grew, it became clear that investors are not just logical beings but are also impacted by social dynamics, emotions, and cognitive biases. For instance, psychological traits like herd mentality, loss aversion, and overconfidence have a big influence on investment choices. Even in the area of portfolio management, these realisations have steadily impacted conventional beliefs. Researchers like Richard Thaler, Amos Tversky, and Daniel Kahneman have produced ground-breaking studies on cognitive biases and decision-making that both support and, in certain situations, contradict traditional economic presumptions. In contrast to the rational, utility-maximizing behaviour assumed in traditional finance, investors are frequently more sensitive to potential losses than equivalent gains. This is explained by prospect theory, which was first proposed by Kahneman and Tversky and highlighted how people value gains and losses differently.

It is crucial to understand that the argument between behavioural finance and traditional finance is more nuanced than is frequently depicted. The two schools of thought have begun to merge more and more. In order to better explain investor behaviour and market oddities, behavioural elements have been added to financial models over time. For instance, behavioural economics has offered empirical support for comprehending irrational behaviour in market environments, and modern portfolio theory has developed by recognising the influence of investor psychology on risk and return. Because it considers both the psychological aspects of human behaviour and the mathematical models of classical finance, this convergence is crucial for a more thorough understanding of financial markets. It provides a more comprehensive picture of investor decision-making and market efficiency.

In this situation, using behavioural finance becomes essential for addressing some of the shortcomings of conventional theories as well as for enhancing our comprehension of market dynamics. Behavioural finance takes into consideration the human factor, which is crucial in explaining why markets occasionally defy efficiency and logic, whereas EMH presents an idealised, logical picture of market players. Navigating the intricacies of contemporary investing will require an awareness of these behavioural and psychological aspects as markets continue to change due to the growing impact of social media and technology developments.

But markets are sometimes predictable. The dot-com boom of the late 1990s served as a stark warning that markets can and do derail. Investors ignored rationality and poured money into computer businesses merely because their names included ".com." There were firms with no profits, no clear business strategy, and, in some cases, no actual products—but their stock values skyrocketed. If the EMH were genuine in its purest form, we would not witness bubbles like this. The theory gives a framework for understanding why markets tend to become more efficient over time, but it fails to explain the irrational frenzy that seems to defy rationality. Nonetheless, EMH has significant benefits, notably in explaining why it is so difficult for even the most experienced specialists to regularly outperform the market—why, despite all of their abilities and equipment, even professional fund managers sometimes fail to "beat the street."

Modern Portfolio Theory and CAPM

Then there is Modern Portfolio Theory (MPT), which Harry Markowitz created in the 1950s. MPT urges investors to consider risk as well as reward. Markowitz maintained that an investor's best strategy is to diversify their investments over a variety of baskets—some dangerous, some safe. This allows them to lower their total risk without compromising returns. Consider a farmer who raises many crops, such as corn, wheat, and soybeans. If one crop fails due to adverse weather, the others may flourish, helping the farmer to reduce losses. In financial terms, this entails diversifying investments over many assets so that if one underperforms, the others may help soften the impact. The theory developed the notion of the efficient frontier, which is an imaginary line that represents portfolios with the highest feasible return for a given degree of risk. In reality, MPT is the foundation of what financial consultants offer to their clients: a portfolio of stocks, bonds, and other assets that balance risk and return (Markowitz, 1952).

The Capital Asset Pricing Model (CAPM) emerged to take things a step further. CAPM allows an investor to determine how much return they should anticipate based on the degree of risk they are incurring. It is a formula that takes into consideration the risk-free rate (such as the return on a government bond, which is regarded as nearly risk-free), the asset's beta (which quantifies how much it swings in relation to the general market), and the anticipated market return. In layman's words, CAPM explains what type of payoff you can expect for taking on a specific degree of risk. It functions as a road map for investors, assisting them in determining if the prospective return on an investment is justified by the risks involved. CAPM allowed us to quantify risk and reward, establishing a mathematical link between how hazardous an investment is and the expected payout. It is a fundamental component of conventional finance, used to value anything from equities to real estate.

But here is when everything begins to unravel. Traditional models like as EMH, MPT, and CAPM all make significant assumptions: that investors are rational, have all of the information, and utilise that knowledge objectively. But consider real-world investors like you and me. Are we always rational? Do we always make choices free of emotion? Think about the 2008 housing market crisis. People purchased properties they could not afford, believing that prices would only rise. Banks made loans to visibly dangerous customers with the notion that they could bundle and market the loans as "safe" assets. Investors purchased mortgage-backed securities that they needed to comprehend because they trusted rating agencies and banks. When the bubble burst, the whole financial system came crumbling down, demonstrating how much reality may deviate from the logical ideal.

What these classic theories overlook is the emotional, psychological, and social aspects of investment. People are not calculators; they are motivated by fear, greed, and a desire to fit in. The growth of behavioural finance stems directly from the limits of classical ideas. According to behavioural finance, in order to really understand markets, we must first understand the individuals who drive them. Why do we pursue hot stocks? Why do people worry when prices drop? Why do we make judgements that, in retrospect, seem entirely irrational? Traditional theories provide a view into the ideal world in which all investors make rational decisions and prices always represent genuine worth. However, behavioural finance offers insight into the real world, where individuals make choices based not just on statistics but also on emotions, stories, and the impact of others around them.

Rising of Behavioural Finance

Behavioural finance offers a framework for analysing such situations. It demonstrates that cognitive biases—mental shortcuts that help us make judgements fast but may also contribute to errors—influence investors' decisions. One of these biases is overconfidence, which causes investors to overestimate their talents while underestimating hazards. During the dot-com bubble, investors believed they could predict the winners of the new digital economy. They felt they had exceptional insight and that they could see the future better than others. This overconfidence caused them to overlook warning indications, disregard established valuation measures, and place large bets on firms that eventually failed. Overconfidence is a tremendous force—it makes us feel invincible, as if we influence results that are, in fact, out of our reach.

Another key topic in behavioural finance is Prospect Theory, which was created by psychologists Daniel Kahneman and Amos Tversky. Prospect Theory questions the conventional wisdom that investors are always rational and utility-maximizing (Kahneman & Tversky, 2013). Instead, it demonstrates how individuals evaluate wins and losses differently. The agony of losing $100 considerably outweighs the joy of getting $100. This is known as loss aversion, and it has a significant impact on investment behaviour. Loss aversion explains why investors often hang onto losing equities for too long—selling would entail locking in a loss, and the emotional anguish of doing so is too high. It also explains why investors rush to sell winning equities in order to "lock in" profits before they evaporate. These behaviours are nonsensical, yet they are fundamentally human (Kahneman & Tversky, 1979).

Consider Susan, an investor who buys stock in a promising technology business. The corporation has a complex spell, and the stock price starts to plummet. Susan assures herself that this is just a short setback, that the firm will rebound, and that selling now is a mistake. Weeks come into months, and the stock continues to drop. Every day, Susan looks at her portfolio and notices the red numbers, but she cannot bring herself to sell. Selling would imply acknowledging a mistake, that she was incorrect about the company's prospects. The emotional weight of that realisation is too much for her to bear, so she clings on in the hope of a rebound that never arrives. This is loss aversion in action—the unwillingness to accept a loss, even when it is the logical thing to do.

Traditional finance also believes that investors can evaluate all available information objectively and make judgements based on a thorough examination of probability and outcomes. However, behavioural finance recognises that our cognitive powers are restricted. We utilise heuristics, or mental shortcuts, to make judgements fast. While these shortcuts may be advantageous, they sometimes lead to systemic mistakes. Consider anchoring bias, which occurs when individuals make judgements based on the first piece of information they receive. Consider an investor called Mark who hears a financial expert forecast that a particular stock would hit $150 per share. That amount becomes an anchor in Mark's mind, and despite fresh evidence indicating that the firm is experiencing significant issues, he stays focused on the $150 aim. The anchor distorts his view, causing him to hang onto the stock long after the reasonable choice would be to sell.

Another cognitive bias that influences investor behaviour is the representativeness heuristic. This is the propensity to assess the likelihood of an occurrence based on its similarity to something familiar. During the dot-com boom, many investors recognised similarities between emerging computer businesses and Microsoft or Apple. They felt that merely because they were in the technology area, these firms would achieve similar success. The parallels were superficial, but the representativeness heuristic caused investors to disregard the underlying facts and believe that history would repeat itself. This bias resulted in financial misallocation, as investors poured money into firms with little possibility of emulating the tech giant's success.

Behavioural finance also helps us understand how emotions influence financial choices. Fear and greed are the two emotions that underpin most of the irrational behaviour in financial markets. Greed drives investors to seek profits and buy into rising markets without examining if the values are reasonable. It convinces them that they can get wealthy rapidly and that the chance is too excellent to pass up. Fear, on the other hand, causes panic and rash judgements. When markets tumble, the inclination is to sell and get out before things worsen. This cycle of fear and greed causes volatility as investors fluctuate between joy and terror. Understanding these emotional motivations is critical to making sound investing choices. It requires discipline, self-awareness, and a willingness to face our unreasonable behaviour.

Table 2.1. Key Differences Between Traditional and Behavioural Finance Theories

Topic	Traditional Finance	Behavioural Finance
Core Ideas	Imagine a world where investors are like financial superheroes—logical, informed, and cool-headed. They have all the data they need, use it wisely, and always make the best choices. Traditional finance believes markets work just like that. Prices reflect all available info, so getting ahead of the game? Almost impossible.	Behavioural finance says, "Not so fast." It is more about real humans who make mistakes, feel fear and greed, and follow the crowd. People are not always rational, and neither are markets—they swing with the emotions and quirks of the people who drive them.
Major Theories	**Efficient Market Hypothesis:** The idea that markets are super smart and always "right." **Modern Portfolio Theory (MPT):** Diversify well, and you are set. Risks get spread out! **CAPM:** Think of it as a financial map connecting risk with returns. **Arbitrage Pricing Theory (APT):** Similar to CAPM but more complex—returns are influenced by many things, not just market swings.	**Prospect Theory:** People hate losing more than they love winning. So, they are often risk-averse until they are facing losses, then they take bigger risks to avoid regret. **Mental Accounting:** People make "mental" categories for money and treat it differently based on these imaginary accounts. **Herding:** When the crowd moves, people follow—even if it does not make sense, it feels safer!
View on Market Behaviour	Markets are like calculators—prices change only when there is new information. As soon as news drops, prices adjust. Efficient markets mean no big surprises, and any missteps get corrected fast.	Picture the stock market as a rollercoaster. News, emotions, rumors—they all shake things up. Markets can be downright irrational, with trends and crashes fueled by emotions like fear, greed, and hype.

Investor Mindset	Investors are self-interested but calm thinkers, making decisions purely to maximize wealth, without letting feelings cloud their logic.	Investors are more like everyday folks, prone to bias, mood swings, and a tendency to be overconfident. They might hold onto losing stocks too long or sell winning ones too soon because of feelings, not facts.
Impact on Prices	Prices are practically perfect, meaning any mispricing gets adjusted as soon as someone spots it. The market self-corrects.	Prices can get totally out of whack because of human quirks. Think of housing bubbles, where emotions drive prices way above actual values.
Risk and Reward	More risk, more reward. But that risk is always measured and calculated, with rational decisions keeping things on track.	People often react more strongly to potential losses than equivalent gains, leading to choices that can defy logic. Sometimes they take more risks just to "break even" after a loss.
Investment Strategies	Diversify, diversify, diversify. Pick low-risk stocks to balance high-risk ones. Passive investing wins because outsmarting the market is not likely.	Investors may take on bolder strategies like "contrarian" investing (buying what everyone else avoids) or "momentum" investing (chasing recent winners) because emotions drive choices as much as rational planning.
Criticisms	Critics say traditional theories ignore human nature. People are not perfect decision-makers, and the real world is full of shocks and surprises.	Some say behavioural finance cannot always predict what people will do next. Emotions vary widely, and it is hard to nail down exact formulas for irrational behaviour.
Examples in Action	Think of models like EMH or CAPM, where everything from pension funds to investment banks uses these concepts to guide decisions. But real crises like 2008 showed these models sometimes miss the mark when investor behaviour goes haywire.	Behavioural finance explains booms and busts, like the tech bubble, where people got swept up in hype, or the 2008 crisis, when herd mentality played a huge role. Efforts to "nudge" better decisions, like financial education, are part of the behavioural finance toolkit.

Source: Author's Work

The contrast between conventional and behavioural finance is essential to our understanding of investor behaviour and market dynamics. Traditional finance theories have long moulded our understanding of markets, predicated on rationality, efficient information processing, and calculating decision-making. These theories, such as the Efficient Market Hypothesis, Modern Portfolio Theory (MPT), and Capital Asset Pricing Model (CAPM), propose that markets function with near-perfect efficiency. In this theory, investors are rational agents that attempt to maximise utility while precisely processing all available information and ensuring that asset prices represent intrinsic values. Any divergence from these values is assumed to be temporary, rectified quickly by rational arbitrageurs who take advantage of brief mispricings. The implications of these ideas are straightforward: market prices represent genuine worth, making it almost hard to consistently beat the market via stock selection or market timing. Critics contend that standard models imply an idealised investor who is unaffected by the psychological and emotional nuances of human nature.

In contrast, behavioural finance offers a more sophisticated, human-centred approach to understanding markets. Behavioural finance arose in reaction to the shortcomings of classical theories, specifically their failure to account for the irrationalities evident in real-world investor behaviour. Pioneers like Daniel Kahneman and Amos Tversky developed ideas such as Prospect Theory, which emphasises that investors do not view profits and losses equally. Losses elicit higher emotional reactions than equal profits, resulting in risk-averse behaviour in the face of wins and risk-seeking behaviour in the face of losses. This "loss aversion" propensity is only one of many cognitive biases, including overconfidence, anchoring, and mental accounting, that behavioural finance theorists believe influence decision-making. According to behavioural finance, investors are affected by heuristics and social influences, which often lead to herding behaviour in which people follow the pack, reinforcing market trends. This deviation from rationality implies that markets are prone to overreaction and underreaction, resulting in asset booms and collapses that classical finance cannot completely explain.

The two theories have radically different perspectives on market efficiency and investor rationality. Traditional finance supports the concept of efficient markets, which maintains that prices respond quickly to new information and represent inherent value. In this perspective, if anomalies occur, prudent investors swiftly exploit them, preserving market stability. However, behavioural finance challenges this assumption, claiming that markets are often inefficient owing to systemic errors in investor psychology. Bubbles, such as the dot-com boom or the 2008 financial crisis, demonstrate how irrational exuberance, fear, and herd behaviour may cause prices to deviate from underlying values, resulting in lengthy periods of mispricing. Behavioural finance theorists see these market anomalies as evidence that prices do not always represent genuine value, and so chances for above-market returns exist, although with increased risk owing to the inherent unpredictability of human behaviour.

Investor behaviour is likely the most significant distinction between conventional and behavioural finance. According to the classic paradigm, investors are rational and self-interested, making choices with the aim of maximising wealth based on objective risk and return estimates. They follow Expected Utility Theory, estimating possible outcomes with accuracy. However, behavioural finance demonstrates that investors are often irrational. Cognitive biases impact their views, and emotions might impair their judgement. Overconfidence, for example, might lead to excessive trading because investors believe they have better information or prediction ability. Similarly, anchoring may lead to investors relying too strongly on the initial piece of information they get, even if later evidence indicates otherwise. Mental accounting, another cognitive bias uncovered by behavioural theorists, demonstrates that people often divide their money into several mental "accounts," handling it differently depending on subjective rather than objective financial rules.

Financial Crises and Behavioural Finance

Consider the Global Financial Crisis of 2008, a contemporary financial disaster caused by unregulated risk, misguided trust, and an apparent misunderstanding of the underlying market hazards. It started in the early 2000s when interest rates were low, credit was plentiful, and everyone, from homeowners to Wall Street giants, was high on the prospect of ever-increasing house values. Financial institutions started granting mortgages to individuals with little or no capacity to repay, known as subprime borrowers. These hazardous loans were subsequently combined into mortgage-backed securities (MBS) and collateralised debt obligations (CDOs). Wall Street transformed them into lucrative assets and branded them as safe investments, persuading worldwide investors of their reliability.

This method was backed by the EMH, which said that financial market prices represented all available information. The hypothesis argued that if these assets were regarded secure, they would be appropriately valued for their risk. The rating agencies in charge of analysing risk assigned AAA ratings, signifying minimal risk, which boosted investor confidence even further. However, this trust needed to be revised since many of these assets included toxic mortgages that would unravel under any economic hardship. When property prices started to fall in 2007, the foundations broke. By September 2008, Lehman Brothers had declared bankruptcy with over $600 billion in assets, causing worldwide fear. The stock market dropped quickly, with the

Dow Jones plunging 54% from its 2007 high, wiping down $19.2 trillion in worldwide family wealth. Banks ceased lending to one another, causing a credit crisis that resulted in 8.7 million job losses in the United States between 2008 and 2010, driving economies throughout the globe into severe recession.

The crisis was more than simply the failure of complicated financial mechanisms; it was also a failure of human nature. Investors, fuelled by overconfidence, overlooked the hazards in quest of quick profits. Nobel winner Daniel Kahneman described this behaviour using Prospect Theory: investors were so focused on rewards that they missed hazards, and their reluctance to admit losses caused them to hang onto assets even as their prices fell. This psychological barrier kept banks, hedge funds, and private investors from reducing their losses until it was too late, exacerbating the crisis. The repercussions were far-reaching: millions of people lost their homes, companies faltered, and unemployment rates rose dramatically across many countries. The supposedly impenetrable global economic system was shown to be a house of cards constructed on human mistakes and misguided hope.

Another dramatic example of conventional banking failing to forecast a disaster was Black Wednesday, which happened on September 16, 1992, in the United Kingdom. The British government's commitment to the European Exchange Rate Mechanism (ERM) included keeping the pound within a set exchange rate range versus other European currencies. The goal was that aligning currencies would promote economic stability and ultimately lead to a single European currency. To preserve the pound's value, the government hiked interest rates to a record 15% and spent billions of pounds from overseas reserves. However, the UK economy was suffering from rising inflation and unemployment, and the high interest rates stretched an already fragile economy.

The issue drew the attention of speculators such as George Soros, who saw that the pound was overvalued and that Britain could not maintain its place in the ERM. In what became one of history's most famous currency deals, Soros started shorting the pound. As additional speculators joined in, the selling pressure became overpowering. Despite the British government's efforts, the market's expectation that the pound would ultimately depreciate became a self-fulfilling prophecy. The UK government left the ERM, enabling the pound to float freely, resulting in its depreciation. The anticipated cost to the UK Treasury was roughly £3.3 billion, and the confidence of the government's economic policy was severely harmed.

Meanwhile, Soros made $1 billion on his gamble. The crisis demonstrated the limitations of government involvement in financial markets. Traditional models anticipated that rational actors would trust government decisions, but instead, investors followed Soros' lead and bet against the pound in large numbers.

The Russian Financial Crisis of 1998 serves as yet another warning of how vulnerable financial institutions may become when exposed to global market volatility and political unpredictability. During the mid-1990s, Russia was undergoing the transition from a centrally planned to a market-oriented economy. To fund significant budget deficits, the government issued short-term, high-yield government bonds (GKOs), banking mainly on growing global oil prices to keep the economy stable. The high yields supplied by these bonds produced strong risk-adjusted returns, according to the Capital Asset Pricing Model (CAPM). For a while, the tactic succeeded, and investors were eager to purchase these high-yield instruments, expecting that the oil-rich government would pay its bills.

However, by 1998, the situation had deteriorated as global oil prices fell precipitously—from $23 per barrel in 1997 to roughly $12 per barrel in 1998. Russia's income declined, making it unable to meet its financial commitments. The government defaulted on $40 billion in debt, and the ruble's value fell by more than 60%. Inflation surged to 84%, and the stock market lost more than 75% of its value, causing widespread economic turmoil. The crisis sent shockwaves across the global financial system, precipitating the collapse of Long-Term Capital Management (LTCM), a prominent hedge fund in the United States, necessitating a rescue engineered by the Federal Reserve to avoid a more significant financial collapse. The Russian default demonstrated the limitations of CAPM and other classic models that assumed that a transitional state's political risks and economic issues were adequately priced. Investors, overwhelmed by availability bias, recalled previous crises in developing economies and immediately withdrew their funds, causing broad financial contagion.

The Latin American Debt Crisis of the 1980s, sometimes known as the "Lost Decade," demonstrated the repercussions of uncontrolled optimism and financial overextension. During the 1970s oil boom, Latin American countries such as Mexico, Brazil, and Argentina borrowed heavily from foreign banks to fund large industrial and infrastructural projects. Traditional financial models saw these loans as rational—interest rates were low, and the return on investment was projected to promote economic activity. However, rather than making profitable investments, most of the borrowed money was directed into inefficient state-owned firms and poorly managed projects. It is also important to note that during this period, many Latin American countries were governed by military dictatorships that exacerbated these issues. The political instability and lack of democratic oversight meant that economic decisions were often made with little regard for long-term stability or sustainable growth. When the US Federal Reserve boosted interest rates in the early 1980s to battle domestic inflation, the cost of repaying these loans skyrocketed. In August

1982, Mexico stated that it could no longer satisfy its financial commitments, triggering a wave of defaults around the region. The lack of political accountability and the financial mismanagement that occurred under these regimes contributed to the severity of the crisis, which not only had devastating economic consequences but also deepened the social and political instability in the affected countries.

The economic consequences were significant. Average GDP growth in Latin America fell to 0.9% for the decade, compared to 5.6% in the 1970s. Inflation rose dramatically, with nations such as Argentina suffering hyperinflation rates of more than 3000% in 1989. Poverty rates rose as unemployment increased, and living conditions plummeted substantially. International banks suffered significant losses, necessitating a concerted rescue effort headed by the International Monetary Fund (IMF). Herding behaviour among foreign lenders intensified the crisis; after Mexico failed, banks anticipated that other nations would soon follow, causing financing to dry up and driving other defaults. The situation worsened, demonstrating the dangerous interdependence of global banking and the implications of overleveraging, especially in developing economies.

The 1997 Asian Financial Crisis was yet another stark reminder of conventional finance's inadequacies when dealing with unexpected fluctuations in market opinion. The crisis started in Thailand, where the economy was quickly expanding thanks to foreign investment and speculative real estate expenditure. The Thai baht was tied to the US dollar, but as the currency rose in the mid-1990s, Thailand's exports grew more costly, contributing to a growing trade imbalance. When investors were concerned about the Thai economy's long-term viability, they started withdrawing funds. Thailand was compelled to float the baht on July 2, 1997, causing a fast depreciation that triggered a domino effect across Southeast Asia.

The chart below, labelled as Figure 2.1, illustrates the changes in stock market performance for Malaysia, Thailand, South Korea, and Indonesia during the 1996-1999 period, highlighting the profound economic impacts of the 1997 Asian Financial Crisis on each of these nations.

Figure 2.1. Stock Market Performance in selected Asian Countries (1996-1999)

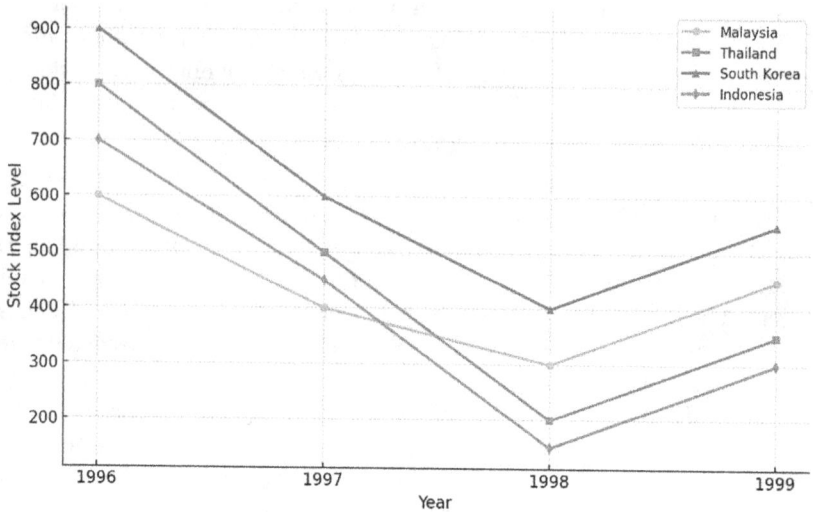

Source: Author's Work

In 1996, these nations' stock markets remained steady, with no substantial changes in index values. However, 1997 saw the start of the financial crisis, with all four countries' stock market indexes falling sharply. Malaysia's stock index fell by nearly 33.3%, showing a sharp sell-off that coincided with rising investor concerns over currency stability and macroeconomic health. Similarly, Thailand, where the crisis began, had a 37.5% drop in its stock market index after the Thai baht's forced devaluation on July 2, 1997. This devaluation caused widespread fear and a swift outflow of foreign investment, resulting in a sharp drop in asset values across the nation. The effect was particularly strong in the real estate and banking industries, which had received substantial foreign investment during the previous years of economic boom.

Indonesia and South Korea both saw large drops in stock indexes, with Indonesia's index plummeting by around 35.7% in 1997. Investor fears about political instability and mounting foreign debt-fuelled this precipitous slump, exacerbating the economic fragility. South Korea, one of Asia's "Tiger Economies," had its stock index collapse by around 33.3% as the government dealt with increasing debt levels and a significant reliance on foreign capital flows. In both countries, the first stock market collapse reflected broad worries about the viability of economic development models that depended primarily on foreign finance.

By 1998, the crisis had spread throughout the region, with Thailand and Indonesia seeing the most substantial stock market declines. Thailand's stock index fell by another 60%, indicating a cumulative loss of investor confidence as the crisis moved beyond currency depreciation to harm actual economic measures such as GDP and employment. Indonesia suffered the most severe consequences, with its stock index dropping by 66.7%. This precipitous drop highlighted the severity of the economic and social issues, which included significant capital withdrawals, a severe devaluation of the rupiah, and consequent political unrest. South Korea's stock index fell by a further 33.3% as the country dealt with debt restructuring and a fast drop in industrial production, which had been the backbone of its economic development.

The year 1999 saw indications of recovery in various nations, although at different speeds. Malaysia's stock index recovered by almost 50% as the government undertook a number of fiscal and monetary measures intended to stabilise the economy, including capital restrictions to prevent speculative assaults on the currency. Thailand's stock index recovered by 75% after major structural changes and IMF backing, demonstrating both local policy improvements and a gradual recovery of international investor confidence. South Korea's index increased by 37.5%, thanks to government-led restructuring measures and foreign financial assistance that helped stabilise the banking system and encourage economic recovery. Indonesia, which suffered the most severe economic and social issues, had a spectacular 100% rebound in its stock index level from the previous year's low, while the economy remained weak owing to continued political concerns.

By the end of 1997, the Thai stock market had fallen 75% in dollar terms, while the Indonesian rupiah had lost 80% of its value. South Korea, formerly considered an "Asian Tiger," had its GDP fall by 5.8% in 1998. In all, $600 billion in foreign money departed the area, plunging millions of people into poverty as unemployment rose and companies failed. Traditional financial models underestimated how interdependent and unstable these economies were underneath their surface-level development. Fearing losses, investors withdrew their cash en masse, resulting in a classic incidence of herding behaviour—where panic in one market spread to others, regardless of underlying economic factors. Robert Shiller, who received the Nobel Prize in 2013, often discusses how narratives drive markets more than evidence; in 1997, the story of failing currencies and collapsing economies fuelled a regional financial collapse. These crises, each distinct in their origins but strikingly similar in their outcomes, show that, although standard financial theories give a systematic method to understanding markets, they often miss the subtleties of human behaviour.

The cultural applicability of behavioural finance is one of its drawbacks. Cultural circumstances can have a substantial impact on investor behaviour and the cognitive biases that influence financial decisions. For example, the collectivist culture that permeates many Eastern cultures frequently clashes with the individualistic character of Western markets. While communal decisions may have a significant impact on investment behaviour in collectivist societies, individual decision-making is frequently given priority in Western financial markets. This discrepancy begs the question of whether behavioural finance theories—which have been developed mostly in Western contexts—can be applied to markets in other cultural situations. Research has indicated that cultural influences significantly influence investment behaviours, as biases such as herding and overconfidence may appear differently in collectivist societies than in individualist ones.

The way that investor behaviour has changed over time is another drawback. Prospect Theory and other behavioural finance theories emphasise how psychological aspects influence decisions in the here and now. However, changes in social norms or generational transitions may cause investor behaviour to evolve over time. For instance, because of their varied socialisation and technological exposure, younger generations—like Generation Z—might not display the same prejudices as older generations. The reality is that behavioural tendencies are flexible, despite the long-held assumption by traditional theories such as the EMH that market players behave in a generally constant manner. Certain behavioural presumptions may be challenged or even refuted by the distinct preferences and risk-reactions of younger generations as they join the market.

The influence of outside environmental elements like regulations, globalisation, and economic crises is another drawback. For example, outside factors, rather than the innate psychological biases identified by behavioural finance, may significantly change investor behaviour during periods of economic instability or financial crises. Traditional behavioural finance theories, for instance, were unable to adequately explain the large herd behaviour that sparked widespread panic during the 2008 financial crisis, which resulted in a near-complete breakdown of confidence in financial markets. External shocks, like as regulation changes or the COVID-19 epidemic, can also influence investor decisions in ways that behavioural finance models do not yet adequately capture, as we continue to observe in the age of global financial interconnection. Even while these outside variables have a big influence, they do not always fit easily into behavioural finance frameworks.

The criticism of behavioural interventions—like "nudging"—that have been put up as ways to enhance decision-making is another element that is sometimes missed in discussions of behavioural finance. Although the goal of nudging, as promoted by Thaler and Sunstein, is to help people make better financial decisions, it has come under fire for perhaps compromising individual autonomy. Critics contend that behavioural therapies frequently encourage paternalistic decision-making rather than taking human autonomy into account. This has sparked questions about whether using behavioural finance to inform policy could result in moral conundrums when it becomes difficult to distinguish between coercion and constructive intervention. Furthermore, detractors such as Gerd Gigerenzer (2015) contend that rather than offering straightforward, logical solutions, over-intervening based on psychological insights might occasionally make the biases that the profession aims to combat worse.

Behavioural finance does not discard conventional finance findings; instead, it expands on them by adding a layer of psychological reality that allows us to understand markets better. It teaches us that although markets may be efficient, they are not necessarily so. They are efficient when investors behave logically but inefficient when emotions and prejudices take control (Thaler, 2015). By identifying these inefficiencies, behavioural finance gives us the skills we need to navigate the market more successfully. It shows us that effective investment is more than simply analysing data and anticipating trends; it is also about knowing ourselves, recognising our prejudices, and finding strategies to reduce their effects.

Chapter 3

The Power of the Crowd: Decoding Herding Behaviour

Imagine entering a thriving art gallery in the midst of the city. The gallery is complete with visitors for a show by a fresh, up-and-coming artist. You need to learn more about art, yet you observe a crowd gathered around a specific artwork. People are nodding in amazement, muttering compliments on its ingenuity, and taking photographs. Soon, you find yourself drawn to the same artwork. You are not sure why—perhaps it is the enthusiasm in the air or the sheer number of people enjoying it—but the picture suddenly seems significant to you as well. The more people come around, the more you realise this must be the highlight of the performance. Before you know it, you have decided that it is actually exceptional, even if you cannot explain why.

This is how herding starts—not with detailed study or individual conviction, but with the subtle effect of the mob. When we are unsure, it is our nature to seek guidance from others. In circumstances when we lack experience or are unclear about what to do, the behaviours of others serve as soothing guidance. Herding is more than a behaviour; it is a survival instinct that evolved over thousands of years. Herding, whether it was following the tribe to safety or mimicking others to develop new abilities, has been critical to human survival. However, in contemporary contexts—such as financial markets—this tendency may lead us astray, causing us to make judgements based on emotion rather than logical thinking.

Behind Herding

In the area of investing, herding occurs when people follow the activities of others rather than doing their analysis. Assume you are a young professional who has just begun investing. You have some funds and have been investigating several firms. One evening, while scrolling through your social media account, you notice that a lot of people are talking about a particular stock—it is trending, and everyone seems to be profiting from it. You will read postings full of enthusiasm, pictures of excellent returns, and even a few success stories of individuals who "made it big" in only a few weeks. The more you browse, the more you feel the weight of everyone heading in the same direction. Suddenly, it seems like you have been missing something. You begin to doubt your judgement—how could so many people be incorrect? You decide to buy in the stock not because you have researched the company's fundamentals but because everyone else is doing it. This is herding—the assumption that there is wisdom in numbers causes us to follow the pack, frequently to our cost.

Herding behaviour in financial markets is primarily motivated by the deeply entrenched human yearning for coherence and belonging. At its foundation, people have an inherent need to align their behaviour with that of a group, which provides a feeling of oneness and alleviates the pain associated with uncertainty (Banerjee, 1992). This is not a deliberate attempt to fit in but rather a subconscious draw towards acts that are consistent with what others are doing. When confronted with ambiguous or difficult circumstances, such as investing in unpredictable markets, people prefer to gaze outward, instinctively associating with the collective, which gives psychological comfort in the face of overwhelming alternatives. The herd's movement sends an implicit signal that there is a common understanding, enabling individuals to disregard personal reservations.

The psychological underpinnings of herding are also tied to cognitive shortcuts, or heuristics, that the human brain employs to simplify decision-making. In financial markets, where information overload is widespread and fast judgements are critical, the brain often relies on signals from the surroundings. When a person notices a significant number of individuals making the same choice, their brain interprets it as a heuristic—a mental shortcut—that the behaviour must be proper or advantageous. It removes the stress of in-depth investigation and critical thought, replacing it with the relative simplicity of following group actions. This is especially true in instances when people feel themselves having less competence than those they are seeing, leading to a stronger propensity to defer to the group.

Another psychological effect of herding is a decrease in perceived personal responsibility. Individuals feel less vulnerable to the repercussions of their conduct when their behaviour reflects that of a bigger group. If the judgement proves to be erroneous, blame is shared, reducing personal culpability. This decentralisation of responsibility may alleviate the stress and anxiety associated with taking financial risks because individuals believe the collective shield of the group protects them. The comfort of not being alone in making a potentially expensive choice is a solid psychological motivation, gently pushing people into herd behaviour without conscious recognition of the underlying mental dynamics.

Herding in markets is a complicated phenomenon, including psychological biases, societal factors, and informational obstacles. One of the primary reasons for herding is social proof. Social proof is the inclination to believe that the behaviours of others represent the appropriate behaviour in a particular scenario. It is a cognitive shortcut that allows us to make judgements without having to consider every element individually. If everyone else is purchasing a stock, it must be a solid investment, correct? Social proof works on a fundamental level: the more people who do something, the more we feel it is the proper thing to do. This is particularly true when we are unsure or need more knowledge to make an educated choice. When we are uncertain, we turn to others for advice, believing they know something we do not.

Consider this hypothetical scenario: you are thinking about investing in biotech, but you need to learn more about it. You enter into an online investment forum and notice a message from a well-known member who has invested in a specific biotech business. The post is informative and confident, and it quickly received hundreds of likes and positive comments. Other members begin to speak out, reflecting the opinion that this firm is a winner, and soon, there is a frenzy of enthusiasm. You have seen that the stock price has been slowly rising over the last several weeks. The fact that so many people are discussing it, all in agreement, makes you believe that this firm is worth investing in. This is social proof in action—the confirmation supplied by the audience persuades you to invest even if you have not done your extensive study. You follow the crowd, confident that the collective knowledge must exceed your doubt.

Another critical source of herding is the fear of missing out or FOMO. The fear of missing out is a strong emotion that drives us to behave, sometimes foolishly, in order to prevent feeling excluded or regretful. In the financial markets, FOMO may be a powerful motivator for herding behaviour. Consider this: your colleague, whom you have always regarded as a mediocre investor, suddenly begins bragging about how much money they have earned by investing in a hot new cryptocurrency. They are overjoyed, showing off their riches on their phone and talking about taking a holiday with the proceeds. Then, another colleague comments that they are also joining in on it. You begin to feel uneasy—not because you are concerned about the hazards, but because you are afraid of losing out on an opportunity that others are taking advantage of. The thought that others are getting money and you might be too is overpowering. Even if you have questions about the investment's authenticity or durability, the fear of being left behind is enough to motivate you to take action. You invest in cryptocurrencies not because you feel it is valuable but because the prospect of missing out is too great to bear.

Confirmation bias, or the propensity to seek out and interpret information in a manner that supports one's previous ideas, is another factor driving herding behaviour. Assume you have heard about an excellent technological company and are enthused about its prospects. You begin seeking information on the firm, and you come across articles and postings from other investors who are similarly hopeful. This validation confirms your opinion that this is an excellent investment. When you see other people purchasing the stock, it seems like further confirmation of what you already think. You overlook any negative information or cautions, instead focusing on positive signals that match your excitement. Herding becomes a technique to justify your judgements since others' behaviours support what you already think.

Emotional contagion is another crucial driver of herding, which occurs when emotions spread across communities, persuading people to adopt similar sentiments. Imagine attending a performance where the whole audience is dancing and singing along (Baker & Wurgler, 2006). Even if you are not a big fan of the band, it is difficult not to be swept up in the enthusiasm. In financial markets, emotional contagion works similarly. When there is broad enthusiasm for a specific stock, it may spread like wildfire. Investors feed off one another's emotions, escalating the excitement until it reaches a fever pitch.

Similarly, during a market slump, anxiety and panic spread quickly. When investors see others selling, the anxiety spreads, prompting them to sell as well, worsening the slide. Emotional contagion makes herding behaviour especially effective because it is about more than simply intellectual judgements; it is also about the shared emotional experience of being part of a group.

Types of Herding

Reputational herding is all about image, the pressure to maintain one's status in the eyes of others. Imagine yourself as a fund manager whose whole career is based on providing outcomes to customers. You observe that other notable managers are entering a trendy new area, such as biotech or electric cars. You are sceptical. You are aware that these industries have previously had large price fluctuations, and you are sceptical that the fundamentals justify the present values. But the stakes are enormous. If the industry continues to grow while you remain out, your customers will expect explanations. They will wonder why you squandered an opportunity that every other manager seems to recognise. The anxiety of seeming foolish—of falling behind your peers—is tremendous. So you follow the crowd, not because you have changed your opinion about the worth of the assets, but because the reputational risk of missing out is too severe. This kind of herding is not about maximising gains; instead, it is about safeguarding your position and ensuring that you are not the only one standing alone if things go well. It stems from the concern that being different, even if correct, may jeopardise one's job.

In contrast, informational herding is the practice of finding comfort in numbers in the face of uncertainty. Imagine you are at a dinner party, and everyone begins chatting about a particular stock. Some of the visitors seem knowledgeable—perhaps one works in finance, while another has conducted significant study. They are all purchasing and are pretty enthusiastic. You listen to their explanation, which seems persuasive. You do not have the same degree of knowledge, but you start to suspect that they could be on to something. After all, if these people—people you respect—are doing this, maybe you should as well. This is known as informational herding, which holds that others must have knowledge that you do not. It is the comfort of believing, "If they are all doing it, they must know something that I do not." It is a shortcut, a means to escape the uncertainty of choosing without comprehensive knowledge. The problem is other individuals may be thinking the same thing. They may not have more knowledge than you, and their investment choice may be influenced by what they see others doing. The consequence is a chain reaction—a herd established not on solid facts but on the idea that someone else must undoubtedly know the truth.

Then there is institutional herding, which occurs when the major players—banks, hedge funds, and pension funds—start moving in unison. Institutional herding is often motivated by the structure and incentives of the financial sector. Consider a portfolio manager who is required to report on their performance quarterly. The pressure to produce short-term outcomes is enormous. If other institutions are investing in a particular market trend, such as technology stocks or cryptocurrency, the portfolio manager may feel obligated to do the same. Not following the trend might mean failing in comparison to peers, which could result in the loss of customers, bonuses, or even their jobs. Institutional investors tend to herd together since they have access to comparable research and analysis. They all have access to the same analysts, financial models, and market data. This shared knowledge may lead to a convergence of viewpoints, resulting in coordinated behaviour across institutions. When one institution makes a significant move, others swiftly follow suit, not wanting to fall behind or look out of sync with the larger market. This may cause tremendous waves in the financial markets, similar to a big school of fish swimming in tandem, causing turbulence that more minor participants are unable to avoid.

Imagine yourself in a busy neighbourhood on a Saturday afternoon. There is a new bakery around the block, and as you go by, you see a small throng gathering outside. People are conversing, and the queue is expanding. You had not meant to purchase anything, but the sight of that queue piques your interest. "Maybe they are selling something incredible," you will say. You do not even need to know what they are selling; simply watching the enthusiasm and people lining up is enough to pique your interest. Before you know it, you have joined the queue, swept up in the communal excitement. This is herding—a very average human propensity to follow what others are doing, particularly when we do not know what to do ourselves. There is a vital comfort in knowing you are not alone in your choice, in assuming that if so many people agree on something, it must be valuable.

Now consider another situation. This time, you are in the same neighbourhood, but let us look at the psychology of why people are queuing up. The first person may have joined out of curiosity, or maybe they heard that the bakery was giving out free samples. The second individual, seeing the first one join, assumes there must be a cause and follows suit. By the time the third, fourth, and fifth persons arrive, no one is really wondering what is going on. They are merely presuming that those who arrived earlier have valid reasons. This is an information cascade—a chain reaction of judgements made without regard for individual knowledge or analysis, but with the expectation that the actions of those ahead of you would be based on reliable information. People sequentially make choices, with each new person placing greater weight on the decisions of those who came before them than on their private knowledge.

The contrast between herding and information cascades may seem subtle, but it is critical, particularly in understanding financial markets and human behaviour. Herding refers to the general behaviour of following the herd, which is driven by an emotional desire to fit in or a fear of being excluded. When investors purchase a stock because they observe many others doing so, it is often motivated by a primitive need for social proof. There is comfort in numbers, a notion that the crowd's collective knowledge must be correct. Herding occurs because individuals want to be a part of the movement. After all, they think there is safety in numbers and because making a mistake seems less hazardous if everyone else is doing the same thing. Herding may be observed in a variety of contexts, including fashion trends and viral social media challenges. In financial markets, the same dynamic causes bubbles, as consumers pour money into stocks or assets just because everyone else is.

In contrast, information cascades are more delicate and deliberate. Assume you are deciding whether or not to invest in a new technological business. You have done some research but are still determining. You join an investing forum and find that several well-known investors have already invested. You assume they have access to knowledge you do not. Perhaps they know something significant about the company's prospects—maybe they have heard a rumour or have insider knowledge. Despite your doubts, you choose to follow their example. This is not just about the emotional pull of following the herd; it is a deliberate choice to prioritise what you consider to be someone else's superior knowledge. In an information cascade, each individual makes a choice based on the belief that those who came before them had valid reasons for their actions (Bikhchandani et al., 1992). It is less about feelings and more about inference: if others are purchasing, they must know something I do not.

The issue emerges when individuals initiating the cascade act on incomplete or erroneous information, resulting in a domino effect in which everyone feels they are behaving logically, but, in fact, the whole premise for their choice is wrong.

Herding and its Consequences

The dot-com boom of the late 1990s and early 2000s is one of the most vivid instances of speculative frenzy in contemporary financial history. This time witnessed a substantial deviation from conventional investing standards, owing to investors' fascination with new technologies and their potential to influence the future. A few early investors, particularly notable venture capitalists and industry insiders, poured large sums of money into internet firms, laying the groundwork for the boom. These organisations, although frequently lacking long-term income streams or clear profitability prospects, were powered by massive increases in user engagement and market reach, which investors mistook for actual economic value. The early excitement and investments of these well-known persons created a sense of legitimacy in the industry, giving the impression that these pioneers had unique insights into the future worth of internet-based firms.

Figure 3.1. Market Performance During the Dot-Com Bubble (1995-2002)

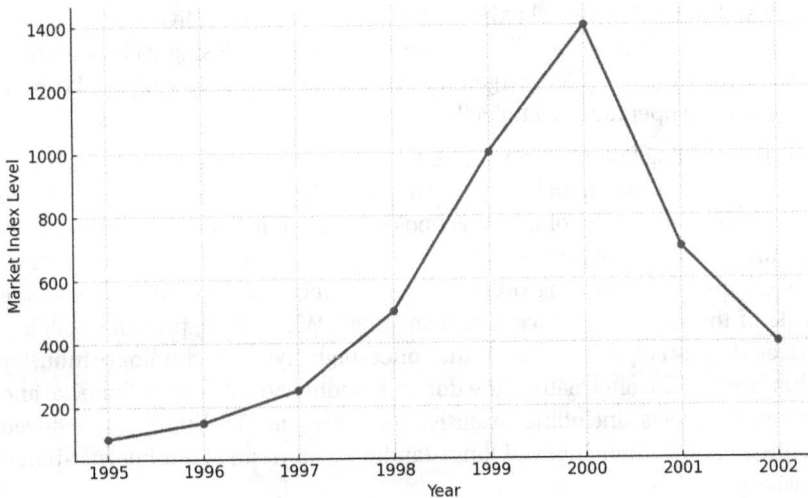

Source: Author's Work

As additional investors witnessed the early, high-profile adopters, an information cascade started to emerge. Rather than independently evaluating the financial realities or commercial feasibility of these firms, prospective investors relied on the assumed expertise of previous investors. This herd behaviour resulted in a surge in stock values, with tech-heavy indexes rising by hundreds of percentage points in a few years. For example, from 1995 to the peak in 2000, the NASDAQ Composite index, which was dominated by technology companies, increased by more than 1,200%, reflecting not just the initial euphoria but also a rising wave of speculative purchasing. Investors came to believe that the exponential price rises represented fundamental worth, sustaining the cycle. For many, the issue of these companies' long-term survival had given way to the notion that fast price increase implied the stocks were valued. This mindset drove prices higher, resulting in a self-fulfilling loop in which rising values attracted more money, while growing demand pushed valuations even higher.

By the bubble's height in early 2000, internet company values had become massively inflated, with price-to-earnings ratios hitting historic highs or, in many instances, firms having no profits to support their stock prices. The final decline began softly, as some investors began to doubt the sustainability of these high values and saw that many of these companies were unlikely to attain profitability. As scepticism crept into the market, the information cascade unravelled. The bubble burst violently, causing a market drop of historical proportions. From its high in March 2000 to its low in October 2002, the NASDAQ Composite fell by about 78%, wiping away billions of dollars in market value and shattering portfolios based on speculative bets. Individual technology stocks had much sharper falls, with several businesses losing 90% or more of their market value, while a large number of online startups went bankrupt or discontinued operations completely.

This cascading failure demonstrated the vulnerability of investor psychology and the potency of herd behaviour in compounding both positive and downward trends. The enthusiasm for a new technology frontier first encouraged investors, but when market sentiment reversed, fear erupted. Investors who had previously felt comfortable following others' investing decisions started to realise the scale of the speculative excess (Odean, 1998). With selling pressure building, prices fell precipitously, and the once-high-flying technology industry plummeted. The aftermath of the dot-com boom had substantial financial and economic effects, including extensive job losses in IT enterprises, reduced venture capital financing, and long-standing scepticism about internet-based business models.

The dot-com bubble's early phases provide a typical illustration of an information cascade in motion. In the late 1990s, a few essential venture capitalists and early investors began investing in Internet startups. It was a new, exciting field, and many of these firms were fast expanding in terms of user base but needed more income. The first investors, many of whom were prominent personalities in the technology business, were regarded as visionaries.

Others followed suit, not because they understood the technology or believed in the long-term viability of these firms, but because they imagined these insiders knew something they could have done better. As more individuals invested, the price of these stocks began to climb, reinforcing the assumption that they must be valuable. The ultimate consequence was an information cascade, with each new investor relying on the perceived wisdom of those who came before them rather than doing their independent study. It became evident that many of these enterprises were unprofitable and needed a clear route to profitability. The cascade failed, and the bubble burst, resulting in huge losses.

The ARKK (Cathie Wood) fund during the post-COVID boom is a recent illustration of herding behaviour in the financial markets. Focussing on innovative, high-growth technology, ARKK became one of the most popular funds among investors as the global epidemic sparked an unprecedented rush into technology equities. Individual investors were enthralled by Cathie Wood's audacious forecasts regarding the future of sectors, including artificial intelligence, genomics, and electric vehicles. ARKK's performance surged, and its popularity skyrocketed as the market recovered from the initial shock of COVID-19, especially among retail investors keen to profit from the "next big thing."

The fear of missing out on the quick profits that ARKK was providing was the driving force behind this herd mentality. Without properly comprehending the risks involved with such volatile investments, many investors poured money into Wood's fund after being enticed by its success tales and seemingly unstoppable development. However, the value of many of the high-growth stocks in ARKK's portfolio fell sharply by 2021 and 2022 as interest rates started to increase and the speculative bubble began to burst. Due to the emotional contagion of the previous enthusiasm, many investors persisted in holding onto their positions, fearful that selling would mean losing out on a possible rebound. A recent example of how herd behaviour, motivated by social proof and FOMO, may lead to large groups of investors ignoring basic risks and following the herd, frequently to their harm, is the ARKK case. This dynamic can result in asset mispricing, volatility, and large losses when the general euphoria wanes, much like in past speculative bubbles.

Herding was also evident throughout the dot-com boom but in a different flavour. It was not just about presuming others had more knowledge; it was about the thrill of being a part of a movement, the dread of losing out on the next great thing. Investors were not simply following others because they felt they had inside information; they were also motivated by social proof, the belief that everyone else was becoming wealthy and that they would be left behind if they did not join in. The psychological pull of herding was enormous.

People witnessed their neighbours, coworkers, and even taxi drivers bragging about their stock profits, and the emotional yearning to be a part of the success narrative grew too great to ignore. Herding during the dot-com bubble was about belonging and participating in communal ecstasy.

Information cascades may look sensible on the surface, but they are based on flimsy foundations. Let us picture a room full of investors bidding on a rare, untested biotech patent. The first investor, sometimes motivated by a gut feeling or a hunch, makes a big offer. Without much time to analyse, the second investor feels the first bidder saw something important and raises his price. The third investor, witnessing two confident offers, believes that this is a fantastic opportunity—two experienced bidders cannot be wrong. This cascade continues, and the patent quickly sells for considerably more than its inherent worth just because each subsequent bidder imagined the prior bidders knew something they did not. The fundamental issue is that no one knows anything meaningful; everyone assumes that the others have done their study. It is a chain reaction in which everyone's choice is predicated on the incorrect assumption that someone else has more knowledge.

The distinction between herding and information cascades may be necessary for understanding how market events occur. Herding often results in bubbles, in which prices soar much above what fundamentals would support, fuelled by the collective passion of the crowd. However, information cascades may lead to a false feeling of certainty, in which everyone feels they are making a reasonable choice based on the supposed knowledge of others. In both circumstances, the risk stems from the fact that the group's decisions are based on assumptions about what others know or think rather than individual solid analysis. This creates a risky scenario in which the whole market may become susceptible since everyone is effectively making the same judgement based on insufficient or inaccurate information.

In financial markets, the interaction between herding and information cascades often results in systemic danger. When investors herd together, they move in the same direction, exaggerating market trends—whether upward or downward—far beyond what underlying economic facts may justify. Knowledge cascades add another layer of risk by creating a veneer of logic, persuading investors that their choices are based on solid knowledge when, in reality, they are just following a chain of conclusions that may be erroneous from the start. Recognising the distinction between herding and information cascades is more than just a theoretical exercise; it is a critical ability for investors looking to escape the traps of collective behaviour. It requires the capacity to analyse the reasons driving market movements and to critically evaluate whether actions are based on actual value or merely the weight of others' judgements.

Herding may have profound effects, including asset mispricing, bubbles, and, ultimately, collapses. Let us take another hypothetical situation. Assume there is a tiny company producing a new kind of electric scooter. Several well-known venture investors invest early, and the business receives some media exposure. Soon, enthusiasm grows as people discuss how these scooters will revolutionise urban transportation. The stock price starts to rise, not because of a considerable advance in the company's technology or profitability, but because an increasing number of individuals are buying in, fuelled by enthusiasm. The firm has become a market darling, with experts on television discussing its "limitless potential." The price climbs, and as it does, more investors want in. However, behind the surface, the corporation is dealing with manufacturing delays and regulatory concerns. These issues are overlooked since the herd is in full gear, driving the price higher and higher. Eventually, the firm needs to catch up on essential milestones, and the enthusiasm evaporates. Investors begin to sell, the price plummets, and those who purchase at the high suffer significant losses. The bubble explodes, and the herd that had rushed forward now flees.

Herding might also cause higher market volatility. When investors act autonomously, they make judgements based on a wide range of information, resulting in a more balanced market. However, when herding takes control, everyone begins moving in the same way, exacerbating price fluctuations. When the crowd buys, prices may skyrocket, frequently beyond what the fundamentals would support. When the herd begins selling, prices might fall rapidly, resulting in significant drops. This kind of behaviour produces boom-and-bust cycles, which may be disruptive to both individual investors and the economy as a whole.

Individuals who engage in herding behaviour may also face psychological effects. Consider Tom, an investor who gets swept up in the euphoria around a particular investment. He sees others purchasing, hears tales of individuals earning enormous profits, and feels compelled to join in. He invests, and for a time, everything goes well—the price rises, and he feels justified in his choice. But then things take a turn. The price begins to decline, and the confidence that comes with being part of the crowd fades. He feels alienated and confused about what to do. The same herd that once comforted him now gives no support as everyone scrambles to sell and reduce their losses. Tom is filled with sorrow, not just because he lost money but also because he knows he did not make the right option based on his analysis. He followed the mob and is now suffering the consequences.

Herding behaviour is sometimes illogical; in some instances, following the herd makes sense. Moving to safer assets, for example, might be a prudent option during times of significant market uncertainty, such as a financial crisis. Suppose there is widespread panic, and the majority of investors are turning to government bonds or cash. In that case, it may be prudent to follow suit, mainly if you are worried about safeguarding your wealth. The difficulty arises in determining when herding is based on facts and when it is just the consequence of emotion or supposition. The difficulty is that most of the time, herding happens in settings when the reasons for collective behaviour are unclear, and the comfort of following the crowd exceeds the need for individual thinking.

Herding behaviour is commonly seen in financial markets when investors follow the herd instead of using their own judgement, a decision that is frequently motivated by uncertainty. Although this may seem illogical at first, herding is frequently a sensible reaction to ambiguous situations. In situations where individual knowledge or experience is inadequate, it turns into a psychological mechanism that offers solace in numbers. People naturally look to others for clues when there is a lot of uncertainty because they believe that the group's combined expertise may be more valuable than their own. This dynamic can be especially noticeable during times of market turbulence when, even when the underlying facts are not completely grasped, the security of following a visible trend offers reassurance.

The seventeenth-century tulip frenzy is a well-known historical illustration of herding behaviour. Due to societal influence and popular speculation, the value of tulip bulbs skyrocketed at this time. The rising prices appeared to validate the investment as more people entered the market, supporting the notion that these prices were sustainable. However, a speculative bubble resulted from this group's enthusiasm, which was predicated on the idea that others had insightful information. When the underlying value was eventually determined to be nonexistent, the price of tulips plummeted, resulting in significant losses for numerous investors. Similar to this, investors flocked to internet companies whose stock values soared despite the absence of strong financials during the tech bubble of the late 1990s. Here, the perceived expertise of early adopters and the fear of missing out led to a chain reaction of investment choices that were not grounded in the true worth of businesses but rather in the conviction that others were more knowledgeable.

Because herding magnifies market movements in both directions, what frequently starts as a basic desire to fit in during uncertain times can have serious economic repercussions. Sometimes, people's objective reasoning is obscured by the emotional pull of following the crowd, which causes them to act impulsively. But herding can also be a sensible approach to decision-making when there is a lot of ambiguity or market misunderstanding. People who follow the crowd are protecting themselves from the unknown by making sure they don't fall behind as others act based on what appears to be insider information. As a result, the relationship between one's own judgement and outside cues is complicated; whereas herding may appear to be a foolish reaction at first, it is frequently a useful adaptation in risky and uncertain situations. Knowing this dynamic makes it easier to understand why, despite the dangers, herding is ingrained in human nature and influences financial markets during both boom and bust times.

Another subtle but crucial consequence of herding is the impact on innovation and capital allocation. Misallocation of resources occurs when investors crowd into a particular industry or asset class. Consider a situation in which renewable energy becomes the hottest new industry, with everyone investing substantially in solar and wind enterprises. While renewable energy is unquestionably vital, the herd mentality may result in excessive valuations for firms that need more solid business models or sustainable practices. Meanwhile, other potentially vital areas, such as water conservation technology or healthcare breakthroughs, need help attracting investment since all emphasis is focused on renewable energy. As a consequence, funding needs to be distributed correctly, and potentially transformational ideas in other areas still need to be funded.

Herding has a considerable effect on market stability. When everyone is heading in the same direction, markets may become highly correlated, which means that various assets begin to move together. The absence of diversity raises systemic risk. Suppose a shock occurs in one section of the market. In that case, it may swiftly spread to others because of the interconnection generated by herding, which creates ripple effects across the financial system. This was obvious during the 2008 financial crisis when herding into mortgage-backed securities caused systemic vulnerabilities that extended across the global economic system when the housing market collapsed.

The environment and socioeconomic elements particular to various nations and cultures have a big impact on investor behaviour. Cross-national research has shown that sociological, cultural, and economic variations can significantly influence investing choices. For instance, because of a culture that values independence and entrepreneurship, individual investors in Western nations— especially the US—tend to exhibit higher levels of risk tolerance and a larger reliance on speculative behaviours. On the other hand, because of collectivist cultures that value prudence and long-term stability, investors in many Asian nations, like China and Japan, tend to exhibit more cautious investment tendencies.

Due in part to less stable financial systems and restricted access to a variety of financial instruments, investors may display higher degrees of herding and risk aversion in developing market nations like Brazil and India. These economic and cultural disparities have a big impact on how investors deal with uncertainty, which can lead to the emergence of various investment biases or worsen herding. In the United States, for example, social proof—observing others invest—may encourage aggressive stock market speculation. However, in more risk-averse nations, the same behaviour may lead to market stagnation or underinvestment, as investor decision-making is dominated by uncertainty and fear of loss.

Furthermore, a country-specific examination shows how investor psychology is influenced by regulatory regimes. For instance, in the United States, a very liquid market and the predominance of investor optimism during bull markets can intensify herding behaviour. Stricter restrictions, like those in some European countries, may cause people to react to market developments more measuredly, which could limit growth but also discourage speculative activity. Divergent tactics and risk-taking behaviours result from variations in taxation, government-backed investment plans, and market accessibility, which further affect how investors respond to market signals globally.

Our comprehension of international market dynamics and investor psychology can be improved by incorporating such country-specific aspects into the examination of investor behaviour. This emphasises how crucial it is to take into account both personal prejudices and the larger socioeconomic context in which investors function. We can learn more about how local circumstances influence global financial patterns and even modify investment plans by comparing behaviours across other locations.

It is crucial to remember that the 2008 financial crisis will be covered in more length in the upcoming chapter, which will give further context for the earlier reference to it. An important illustration of how herding behaviour, driven by overconfidence, inadequate risk assessment, and a general disdain for the underlying economic reality, resulted in a worldwide financial disaster is the 2008 crisis. The financial markets' herd mentality, which led to huge asset mispricing as a result of investor enthusiasm for mortgage-backed securities and other hazardous financial products, is directly responsible for the crisis. Due in part to this herd mentality and a failure to evaluate the risks involved critically, large financial institutions failed, causing significant economic turmoil. The details of the 2008 crisis, the actions that caused it, and the lessons that may be learnt from this disastrous incident will all be covered in the upcoming chapter.

It is significant to take into account economist Anwar Shaikh's work on George Soros' theories in addition to the herding behaviour dynamics seen during the 2008 financial crisis, especially in relation to reflexivity, path dependence, and disequilibrium dynamics. In his 2010 paper "Reflexivity, Path Dependence, and Disequilibrium Dynamics" (Journal of Post Keynesian Economics), Shaikh examines how the market's view of reality can influence real economic outcomes, generating feedback loops that feed speculative bubbles. According to Soros' theory of reflexivity, investors' opinions about the market have the power to directly affect the market, which in turn affects investors' opinions, starting a vicious cycle. Shaikh's work expands on this concept by demonstrating how the opinions of market participants—which are frequently influenced by herd mentality—can skew the actual economic fundamentals, resulting in disequilibrium and market instability. This knowledge is especially important when looking at the herd mentality that occurred during the 2008 financial crisis, when a series of financial collapses were caused by collective miscalculations on the stability of mortgage-backed securities, for example. These beliefs' reflexive character demonstrates how economic crises, like the 2008 crash, are influenced by both external shocks and the self-fulfilling prophecies generated by the psychology of collective investors. This theoretical framework provides a greater understanding of how market outcomes are frequently chaotic and unpredictable due to path dependence, the theory that history impacts the course of economic events.

Although herding behaviour frequently results in the creation of bubbles, as was the case during the dot-com boom or the Bitcoin rush, it is crucial to remember that the final consequences of these bubbles can vary greatly depending on the historical period in question. For example, investing in a bubble at its height could appear foolish in the short run, especially as prices eventually plummet and losses increase. Nonetheless, such investments may still turn a profit, provided a long-term investment horizon is maintained. Over the course of several years, early investments in these equities have proven to be extremely profitable since, for instance, several of the businesses that laid the groundwork for the dot-com boom, like Amazon and eBay, have since achieved notable long-term success. Similar to this, Bitcoin's early years were characterised by high volatility and precipitous price drops, but as the cryptocurrency gained traction in the years that followed, investors who stuck onto their assets experienced significant profits. This emphasises how crucial it is to take into account both the time horizon over which an investment is kept as well as short-term market trends and crowd behaviour. Temporary losses may result from the mentality of the crowd, which can push prices to unsupportable heights, but these volatile times can also present worthwhile chances for long-term investors who stick to a disciplined approach.

Rational or Irrational?
The Truth About Herding

Herding is more than a pattern; it is a ballet of psychology, incentives, and terror that takes place on the stage of financial markets. It is what occurs when a large number of people, each with their dreams and worries, begin to move in the same direction, sometimes without realising why. What makes herding both intriguing and hazardous is that the behaviour itself may fluctuate between logical and irrational, blurring the borders such that even the most experienced investors struggle to identify the difference. To properly understand herding, we must dig past the surface and investigate why individuals follow the crowd—sometimes for good reasons, sometimes to their disadvantage.

Assume you are an investor in a hot bull market. The enthusiasm is evident; the media is full of tales of great returns, new market records, and individuals making it big. Your coworkers are investing and watching their portfolios grow, and everyone seems to have that golden touch. You may argue rationally that the fundamentals are solid, that there is positive news driving the market, and that you want to be included. After all, not engaging might result in losing out on benefits that others are earning. In certain situations, herding might seem entirely sensible. The market is surging, the news is excellent, and the audience is visibly optimistic. It makes sense to follow since the herd's path is consistent with the available knowledge. You persuade yourself that there is safety in numbers and that following the herd will protect you from losses. In a rising market, this notion seems to hold—until it does not.

The difficulty develops when herding becomes a shortcut, and individuals start following without evaluating the crowd's behaviour. In bull markets, the movement of the herd may generate a positive feedback loop. As more individuals buy-in, prices climb, attracting additional purchasers. What begins as sensible behaviour may rapidly turn into irrationality. Investors disregard values, dismiss dangers, and rationalise more outrageous prices simply because everyone else is doing so. It is no longer about the fundamentals of the assets; it is about the emotional fulfilment of belonging and the thrill of watching your investments rise. The same seeming rationality in numbers becomes a trap as the mob pushes prices well beyond any realistic measure of worth.

Consider a fictional investor called Sarah. She is naturally cautious, yet during the early 2000s housing bubble, she watched as friends and coworkers profited handsomely from real estate. At first, she was sceptical—how could prices keep growing indefinitely? However, as more individuals purchased and flipped houses for profit, Sarah started to feel the strain. The news was loaded with tales of individuals generating six-figure gains in only a few months. Her pals spoke about purchasing second and third residences like it was the most normal thing in the world. The market seemed unstoppable, and Sarah quickly found herself visiting open homes and submitting bids. She knew the basics did not line up, but the fear of losing out, the herd instinct, was too great. Everyone appeared to be earning money except for her. Prices had already risen by the time she purchased it, and the bubble would not last long. Following the herd looked like a sensible move, but it turned out to be a financial catastrophe.

You are herding, on the other hand, a logical strategy in uncertain markets, especially during times of extreme volatility. Consider yourself in the midst of market volatility, such as a global crisis, when uncertainty is at its highest. Even experienced investors need help to estimate risk in these situations. The market is responding strongly to each new news, and no one seems to have a clear picture of what comes next. You may see institutional investors flocking towards safer assets like cash, gold, and government bonds. They are lowering their risk exposure, and the rest of the market will soon follow suit. In this scenario, herding is a sensible reaction to significant uncertainty, not a pursuit of profits or hype. By following the herd into safer assets, you insulate yourself from the risk of substantial losses. You may not have all of the knowledge, but you recognise that those who move first are more likely to have it, so you should align with them. Herding is about minimising danger and recognising that in times of uncertainty. Collective knowledge may provide the safest route ahead.

Rational vs. Irrational Herding

Rational herding happens when investors follow the herd because their actions are based on reliable information pointing to a real opportunity. Assume a big pharmaceutical firm releases favourable trial findings for a new medicine. The market responds quickly, and investors, seeing the long-term potential of this innovation, begin purchasing the stock. In this case, herding is rational: investors are reacting to fresh information that indicates a shift in the company's future worth. There is a compelling motive to join the mob, and the collective action is grounded in rationality. Investors use the knowledge that early movers may have more visibility or information, making it prudent to align with them. Rational herding happens when investors make judgements that are consistent with the behaviour of others, citing rational reasoning or shared knowledge. In such cases, the choice to follow the herd is motivated by a reasonable assumption that genuine insights guide market participants' aggregate behaviours. Consider this scenario: a pharmaceutical firm completes clinical testing for a novel medicine that demonstrates excellent effectiveness in treating a common ailment. Investors, realising the possible implications of this news, began purchasing the company's shares. Others who see this move may decide to follow suit, believing that the early investors had trustworthy information to justify their actions. This sort of herding is reasonable since it is based on a legitimate cause-and-effect connection, and each investor acts on the same reliable facts.

Another facet of rational herding is its use as a risk management technique in uncertain situations. When the market is volatile, individual investors may need more knowledge or confidence to analyse risks independently. Instead, they use the behaviour of experienced institutional investors or market patterns as a signal. During economic downturns, for example, investors often flee to bonds or gold to protect their holdings. This trend exemplifies logical herding since it is founded on a common belief that certain assets are typically regarded as safe havens. In this case, following the herd is motivated by a rational desire to reduce risk in the face of uncertainty.

However, rational herding may occasionally lead to illogical results when investors need to distinguish between really educated judgements and those motivated just by momentum. For example, during market upswings, early purchases may be motivated by solid financials or an optimistic economic outlook. However, if prices climb, future investors may need to do a different level of study, thinking that the herd knows best. During this shift, logic begins to erode, and the possibility of a speculative bubble develops. Rational herding requires a thorough assessment of when following others is really motivated by primary motives and when increasing costs merely sweeps away the herd.

Warren Buffett's investments in the aviation business during the mid-2010s are a prime illustration of rational herding. Buffett has long avoided the aviation industry, describing it as a "death trap" for investors owing to its past volatility and poor profitability. However, in 2016, Buffett's Berkshire Hathaway started investing in major US airlines such as Delta, American Airlines, and United. By 2019, Berkshire had acquired roughly $10 billion in airline stocks. Investors watched Buffett, a conservative and widely regarded person, make a move that seemed to indicate a shift in industry fundamentals, such as better financial health, industry consolidation, and increased operational efficiency.

This sparked a flood of investment in airline equities, which was initially rewarded with significant gains. According to Bloomberg, airline shares increased significantly between 2016 and 2019, with Delta Airlines' value rising by around 60%. In this scenario, rational herding was a deliberate choice based on reliable information and a reevaluation of industry fundamentals. The herd was following a sensible, educated narrative—the notion that airlines, after substantial structural reforms, were now a more stable and lucrative business. However, when the COVID-19 pandemic struck in 2020, the airline sector faced unprecedented hardships as worldwide traffic plummeted. Buffett subsequently exited from airlines, seeing that the new reality was radically different from what had initially motivated the investment. This demonstrates that even logical herding may have unfavourable consequences when unexpected occurrences drastically alter the terrain.

However, reasonable herding may readily evolve into an irrational panic. Consider a case in which a single piece of negative news causes a precipitous market decrease. Investors begin selling, prices collapse, and a full-fledged panic ensues. The herd acts in unison, selling equities to avert additional losses, typically at prices considerably below intrinsic value. The emotional component comes in—the sight of others selling causes dread, a sensation that something is going on that you need to get away from. It is no longer about rational analysis or risk minimisation; it is about the overpowering desire to avoid becoming the last person to own a depreciating asset. The pace and size of the sell-off amplified the losses, and what began as a sensible adjustment in portfolio strategy rapidly devolved into a disastrous chain reaction of panic selling.

Irrational herding happens when investors make judgements based on others' behaviour rather than robust and reasonable thinking. This sort of herding behaviour is distinguished by a lack of critical evaluation, in which people follow the crowd, thinking that the majority knows what they are doing. However, the judgements need to be supported by logical analysis or a thorough comprehension of the underlying market realities. In these instances, investors tend to dismiss any independent insights or counter-information that would influence them to behave otherwise. Instead, they prioritise matching their behaviour with that of the majority, which often results in mispricing and unstable market dynamics.

Another essential feature of illogical herding is that it often results in collective overreaction or underreaction in the financial markets. Irrational herding amplifies movements, both upward and downward, since people are motivated by the sheer momentum of the group rather than the essential elements that determine value. For example, a tiny piece of positive news may be amplified when more individuals begin to purchase, thinking that everyone else is acting on reliable information, increasing asset values to unsustainable levels. In contrast, during a moment of negative sentiment, irrational herding may cause a cascade sell-off, bringing prices well below their inherent worth.

Such behaviour causes excessive volatility in financial markets because investors respond more to the actions of others than to objective facts.

Irrational herding also suppresses individual judgement by discouraging investors from making judgements that violate market trends. When investors succumb to irrational herding, they often disregard their thoughts, technical analysis, or research. There is an underlying assumption that the collective market understands more than any individual investor. This effect undermines autonomous thinking and results in similarity in investing behaviour. Individual investors are more prone to make judgements in such situations based on social approval than on an educated risk-reward evaluation. As a consequence, illogical herding may allow a diverse collection of market players to share their perspectives, which is crucial for sustaining good price discovery and market stability.

Furthermore, the effect of irrational herding goes beyond individual investors, influencing more significant market dynamics. When herding behaviour becomes prevalent, it causes enormous market distortions, which may lead to the emergence of bubbles or collapses. Because the herd's behaviours are based on a partial examination of fundamental values, prices might wander significantly from their inherent value, resulting in an unstable market environment. When the gap is too great, dramatic corrections occur, often resulting in significant financial losses for individuals who joined the herd without fully appreciating the dangers. This propensity to quick corrections adds to the inherent unpredictability and risk connected with financial markets.

In contrast, irrational herding is generally motivated by emotions such as fear, greed, excitement, or acute fear of missing out. FOMO is one of the most potent psychological motivators for illogical herding. It is that nagging notion that others are making money while you are waiting on the sidelines that drives investors to seize chances before fully comprehending them. The late 1990s dot-com bubble exemplified this behaviour. Investors, both retail and institutional, poured money into online startups with no business strategy, earnings, or even obvious potential. The Nasdaq Composite Index skyrocketed from about 1,000 points in 1995 to over 5,000 by early 2000, fuelled by the assumption that internet stocks were a sure way to riches.

During this time, it did not seem illogical. After all, the internet was a new technology that was transforming the way the world operated. The promise of the latest digital era was so appealing that reasonable analysis took a backseat to enthusiasm and anticipation. Investors were more worried about losing out on the next great thing than about scrutinising balance sheets or challenging company strategies. FOMO pushed asset values much above sustainable valuations, and when the bubble burst in 2000, several firms, like Pets.com, failed utterly. The Nasdaq, which had peaked at over 5,000 in March 2000, fell to under 1,100 by October 2002, wiping away billions of dollars in market value. What began as sensible excitement about a new technology evolved into irrational exuberance, resulting in significant losses for those caught up in the rush.

The line between rational and irrational herding is not always clear at the moment, particularly given the complications of inadequate information and market mood. Investors often need access to comprehensive data, and the market's behaviour might be impacted by variables that are not immediately apparent. Consider the housing market boom, which contributed to the 2008 financial disaster. Mortgage-backed securities (MBS) and collateralised debt obligations (CDOs) were promoted as low-risk, high-reward investments backed up by AAA ratings from major credit agencies. These ratings, along with the perceived stability of home prices, prompted institutional investors to pour money into these products. From 2000 to 2006, the total value of CDOs issued increased from $69 billion to more than $500 billion, indicating broad faith in their safety.

Initially, this swarming behaviour seemed rational—after all, the ratings were high, and homeownership was seen as a reliable base for investing. However, the underlying loans were more dangerous, and many of the investors who bought them had little understanding of the financial instruments. This insufficient knowledge, along with the herd's excitement, resulted in an overvalued market. When house values began to fall, the cascade of mortgage defaults triggered a crisis that almost brought down the entire financial system. The alleged logical herding, fuelled by what investors thought to be trustworthy information, proved disastrous, exposing the thin line that often divides reason from irrationality in financial markets.

Market mood is crucial in both rational and irrational herding, especially in feedback loops. A positive market mood may set off a reinforcing cycle in which prices increase, more investors buy-in, and prices climb again. This feedback loop may make logical herding look more justified as prices rise, confirming the original choice to purchase. However, sentiment-driven price movement may readily detach from an asset's underlying fundamentals, transforming what was previously sensible behaviour into irrational bubble development. Investors purchase not because the asset has inherent worth but because growing prices confirm their choice, resulting in a risky cycle that often ends with a painful correction.

Bitcoin and Irrational Herding

Take the 2017 Bitcoin explosion as one example. Bitcoin rose from less than $1,000 in January 2017 to about $20,000 in December. The surge was fuelled in part by logical considerations: blockchain technology had transformational potential, and early users recognised the value of decentralised money. However, when the price increased, illogical herding took hold. Many individual investors purchased Bitcoin not because they understood the technology but because they wanted to avoid losing out on the fantastic returns that others were experiencing. This fear—this overwhelming impression that everyone else was becoming wealthy—created enormous purchasing pressure, driving prices to unsustainable heights. When the bubble broke in early 2018, the cost of Bitcoin fell to roughly $3,000, leaving latecomers with significant losses. What began as a reasonable conviction in a potential new technology turned into an irrational frenzy fuelled by FOMO.

The logic of herding often depends on the incentives and quality of information directing investors' actions. Rational herding happens when investors follow the crowd because they feel others have better knowledge or insights that justify their behaviour. This behaviour is motivated by a sensible appraisal of the market situation, in which aligning with the herd makes strategic sense given the available facts. For example, an investor may follow institutional investors into a new sector after a government policy change that favours that industry, provided that these institutional players have done extensive research. In this sense, rational herding is defined as a deliberate choice to support the collective movement using solid reasoning and trustworthy facts.

In contrast, illogical herding lacks this level of reasoning and is primarily motivated by emotional reactions such as fear, greed, or the urge to conform. In irrational herding, investors follow the crowd not because they believe the movement is accurate but because they feel forced to behave similarly to others in order to avoid losing out or to find comfort in numbers. Because of its emotional nature, illogical herding is often reactive, with people relying on social signals rather than undertaking independent investigation or analysis. Investors may invest in a hot trend just because they see others gaining, without considering the dangers or if the underlying fundamentals support the asset's price. This kind of behaviour may easily lead to bubbles or collapses since the herd advances in a direction that is not supported by economic reality.

The capacity to review and adjust is the key differentiator. Rational herding entails constant reassessment—it is not only about following others but also about understanding why the herd is moving and determining if the movement is still consistent with trustworthy principles. Rational investors may adjust their strategy when new knowledge becomes available, either keeping with the herd or electing to leave if the initial reasons no longer apply. In contrast, illogical herding lacks flexibility. It is distinguished by an unyielding conviction that the mob must be correct, regardless of changing circumstances or new evidence that shows otherwise. This rigidity is often what leads to unfavourable financial consequences, as illogical herding fails to account for the subtle, dynamic nature of markets, where circumstances may swiftly alter, turning what seemed to be a sensible investment into a dangerous one.

In the fascinating, unpredictable world of investment, herding behaviour is sometimes seen as a double-edged sword, capable of delivering success or catastrophe. The true definition of this difference, however, is whether herding is logical or irrational. But here is the meat of the issue: in real life, the logic of herding is practically challenging to discern while the action is taking place. Often, it is only in retrospect, when the dust has cleared, that we can conclusively establish whether investors were making rational, information-driven choices or succumbing to mass panic. This grey region is where the full intricacy of herding resides, and it is what makes financial markets both thrilling and terrifying.

Consider the investing world to be a bustling metropolis, filled with people rushing to what appears to be the hottest new attraction—let us call it "The Great Opportunity." From the outside, everyone seems to know something, and those who fall behind cannot help but feel an irresistible pull to follow. However, amid the crowd, it is almost hard to tell the difference between those who really comprehend what lies ahead and those who are running merely because everyone else is. In the heat of the action, logical herding might seem to be the same as irrational herding, and the distinctions become evident only after the attraction turns out to be either a profitable opportunity or an empty promise.

Consider Tom, an investor who detects a sharp increase in the price of a specific semiconductor business. The excitement is electric—news of technology advancements, new contracts, and government subsidies seem to depict a positive picture. Tom joins the herd and buys shares, assuming that others are also acting on reliable information. But how can Tom know whether this is rational swarming motivated by actual technology advancements or irrational exuberance fuelled by FOMO, speculation, and surface optimism? In real-time, it is difficult to tell if the fundamentals are strong enough to sustain the hoopla or whether the market is just overreacting. In this scenario, rationality is obscured by the crowd's clamour and excitement.

Rational herding, when done well, is based on reliable information and measured risks. It is following the lead of those with superior insights or data. Alice, a hedge fund analyst, believes that recognised institutional investors would transfer cash into renewable energy equities in reaction to the government's announcement of expanded solar power subsidies. She does study, determines that the legislative changes are likely to have a significant influence on these enterprises, and chooses to invest. But Alice understands, deep down, that uncertainty exists regardless of her interpretation. Only time will tell if this was a sound move based on actual promise or whether the excitement fades as unexpected challenges come. The wisdom of her decision can only be proven in the aftermath when the market's early excitement has either materialised into sustained growth or faded out as another overhyped promise.

In contrast, illogical herding is often motivated by emotional responses and an innate urge to follow the crowd without first determining whether the herd is travelling in the proper path. John, for example, envisions a flood of retail investors flocking to a fashionable new AI startup. The stock price is skyrocketing, and social media is buzzing with excitement—everyone is talking about how AI will alter the world, and this business is reportedly leading the way. Without any serious investigation, John joins in, caught up by the group's energy. But, as in Alice's case, the whole character of John's decision—whether reasonable or not—will be revealed only after the event. If the company's technology becomes innovative, it will seem to be a wise, sensible decision. However, if the firm stumbles, if its technology fails to meet expectations, or if rivals outperform it, John's decision will be exposed as nothing more than an emotional risk.

The truth of financial markets is that investors, even those who believe themselves reasonable, sometimes need more information. Market prices reflect not just fundamentals but also rumours, conjecture, and the sheer force of collective mood. In this chaotic atmosphere, the line between rational and irrational herding is blurred, and even the most experienced investors may find themselves questioning whether their judgements are based on solid information or just following the crowd. Peter, a venture capitalist, decides to invest in an electric car startup after seeing a spate of well-known investors pour money into it. The startup boasts a great staff, excellent technologies, and a rising market. Peter feels he is operating reasonably, but what happens if the market shifts? What if government incentives shift or new rivals emerge? Suddenly, what seemed to be a sensible conclusion might be reframed as adhering to irrational hype.

The challenge of differentiating logical swarming from irrational herding in real-time is what makes investing both exciting and risky. Rational herding requires ongoing monitoring, a readiness to examine assumptions, and the discipline to leave when the underlying reasons are no longer valid. Martha, a fund manager, first follows the herd into a hot biotech investment after a significant breakthrough is reported. She does her study, validates scientific achievements, and then moves forward. However, Martha understands that keeping reasonable entails constantly reviewing the company's growth. If the therapeutic studies fail or regulatory impediments occur, she must be prepared to go, even if the herd continues to grow. This flexibility is what makes rational herding—it is not about mindlessly following the herd but about understanding when the herd is correct and when to deviate.

Herding is more than simply a pattern; it is a complicated dance of psychology, incentives, and fear played out on the stage of financial markets. It is what occurs when a large number of people, each with their dreams, anxieties, and goals, begin marching in the same direction, sometimes without completely understanding why. Herding's exciting but complex character lies in its ability to swing between logical and irrational reasons, blurring the borders until even the most seasoned investors struggle to distinguish the difference. To properly understand herding, we must dig past the surface and investigate the reasons why individuals follow the crowd—sometimes for legitimate reasons, sometimes to their disadvantage.

Herding might seem like the safest option—there is some comfort in knowing you are not alone and that others share your optimism or anxiety. In times of uncertainty, following the herd may seem to be the wisest decision, mainly if those in charge appear to be guided by reliable insights. But, as we have seen, the distinction between logical and irrational herding is sometimes only visible in retrospect, after the excitement has subsided or the collapse has occurred. The issue for any investor is determining when following the herd is a strategic alignment with knowledge and when it is a risky foray into the unknown. Finally, knowing herding is more than simply understanding the mob; it is also about understanding yourself and the psychological dynamics that drive you to follow or diverge when confronted with ambiguity.

Chapter 5

The Confidence Trap: Overconfidence in Investing

Overconfidence is one of the most common biases impacting investors, prompting them to make judgements that do not reflect their actual knowledge or skill levels. This bias is characterised by an overestimation of one's capacity to comprehend markets, anticipate outcomes, and outperform others. While confidence is essential for successful investment, excessive confidence may lead to harmful behaviours such as excessive trading, underestimating risk, and ignoring diversification—all of which can jeopardise long-term financial objectives.

Overconfidence is a common cognitive bias that is firmly ingrained in human psychology. It occurs when people have an overestimation of their talents, expertise, or judgements, which is often unfounded. Psychologists think that overconfidence arises from a basic need for certainty and control. It provides the reassuring illusion that we can foresee and affect events in an unpredictable environment. This bias is pervasive in complicated and unexpected situations, such as financial markets, where individuals must negotiate uncertainty, and trusting in one's talents offers a psychological safety net. While this drive for control is innate in humans, it often leads to people overestimating their abilities, rendering them prone to mistakes in judgement.

One of the most remarkable elements of overconfidence is that it affects both amateurs and experienced professionals. According to research, specialists with extensive knowledge in their respective disciplines may need more confidence as a result of their expertise. The depth of their learning may give individuals a false feeling of mastery, closing their eyes to their limits and the inherent unpredictability of complex systems. This is known as the illusion of knowledge—the notion that having more information immediately correlates with having better judgement. Paradoxically, as one's competence grows, one becomes more prone to overconfidence, often failing to account for the dynamic, interrelated aspects that impact results.

Psychology of Overconfidence

Psychologically, overconfidence causes a distorted perception of prior triumphs and failures. People often ascribe their triumphs to their ability and judgement while blaming failures on external forces beyond their control. This self-attribution bias promotes overconfidence, resulting in a feedback cycle in which favourable events are internalised as proof of greater competence. Over time, this practice fosters an inflated perception of one's ability, even if previous accomplishments were primarily due to chance or favourable conditions. Such cognitive distortions make it difficult for people to appropriately assess their decision-making processes, resulting in a continual overestimation of their ability to traverse complicated, unpredictable circumstances efficiently. The psychological attractiveness of overconfidence stems from the promise of control and certainty—qualities that, although comfortable, may often lead to severe problems in decision-making.

Overconfidence has a subtle allure—it feels powerful, invigorating, and dangerously comforting. Imagine stepping into a world where every choice you make is bolstered by an unshakeable belief in your own judgement. Your brain serves up the perfect cocktail of assurance and optimism, keeping doubts at bay. The reason? Our minds are hardwired to seek out confidence, a sense of control in an unpredictable world, and overconfidence, in particular, gives us a reassuring, albeit false, sense of mastery.

When we succeed, the brain rewards us generously. A rush of dopamine—the brain's own "feel-good" drug—floods our system, reinforcing those neural pathways associated with success. It is like giving our mind a gold star each time things go our way. The more we win, the stronger these connections become, creating an intoxicating feedback loop where confidence begins to feel not just natural, but inevitable. We start to believe that success is not merely the product of good timing or favourable circumstances but a direct outcome of our skill and intuition. Herein lies the foundation of overconfidence: our brains selectively amplify the highs, sidelining any evidence that might contradict this polished self-image.

Our prefrontal cortex, that master of planning and decision-making nestled behind the forehead, is supposed to act as the brain's impartial referee. It weighs options, assesses risks, and keeps impulse in check. But when overconfidence takes the reins, even this region can bend to its will. Imagine you are standing on the edge of a risky decision—a business deal, a significant investment, or a life-changing move. Ordinarily, the prefrontal cortex would sound the alarm, triggering caution and prompting a careful reevaluation. But under the influence of overconfidence, it silences these cues, downplaying risks and amplifying the potential for reward. You feel invincible, even as you march towards the unknown. In the moment, this sense of certainty feels empowering, but it is the very mechanism that blinds you to the possibility of failure.

Adding another layer to this overconfidence tapestry is the brain's anterior cingulate cortex (ACC). This part of our brain, crucial for monitoring errors and ensuring performance accuracy, should theoretically alert us when things go awry. It is like having a mental watchdog that barks at any sign of a misstep. Yet, when overconfidence is running the show, the ACC's influence wanes, as if the watchdog has been silenced. Instead of acknowledging potential pitfalls, our minds become selective, zoning in on any signal of success and filtering out reminders of risk. This suppression of doubt is not just an accidental glitch—it is a purposeful move by a mind craving certainty, ignoring the subtle hints that might suggest we are out of our depth.

Memory, the vault of our life experiences, plays its own tricks when overconfidence sets in. The brain has a peculiar tendency: it hoards positive experiences, basking in the glow of achievements, while conveniently "forgetting" the painful lessons of past failures. This selective recall, known as positive recall bias, becomes a handy tool for nurturing our overconfident mindset. If you were to scan your mental archives, you might find memories that paint a heroic picture—one where your victories stand front and centre, while missteps and failures are faded, mere footnotes in the grand narrative of your life. Every memory reinforces the myth of self-competence, each one a building block in a psychological fortress that tells you, "You have got this. You have done it before; you can do it again." And so, overconfidence becomes a comfortable echo chamber, with each past success reinforcing a belief in future triumphs.

But why does this bias persist, even when the stakes are high? From an evolutionary standpoint, overconfidence may have been a survival tool. In the wild, a healthy dose of self-belief could have driven early humans to face challenges head-on, whether it was hunting dangerous prey or exploring unknown territories. Confidence, even overconfidence, was a way of overriding fear, allowing our ancestors to press forward when hesitation could mean missed opportunities. The amygdala, the brain's fear centre, plays a role here by regulating the level of threat we perceive. In overconfident states, this region dials down the sense of risk, allowing us to take bold steps forward. In today's world, though, where complex and interconnected systems like financial markets and business landscapes replace the physical threats of the wild, this evolutionary trait can lead us astray. We feel the same primal urge to act boldly, yet the consequences of modern overconfidence are far less forgiving.

And then there is the seductive promise of control, the underlying allure that makes overconfidence so addictive. Our minds crave certainty in a chaotic world, and overconfidence gives us that illusion. It is a safety net woven from pure belief, a mental trick that convinces us we are steering our own ship even as the tides shift beyond our control. In fields that are especially unpredictable, like the stock market or high-stakes negotiations, overconfidence grants us a comforting escape from the anxiety of uncertainty. We embrace the illusion, building elaborate mental castles of "I know what I am doing" and "I have seen this before," even when the foundation is shaky at best.

But the paradox of overconfidence is this: while it bolsters us with a sense of mastery, it ultimately exposes us to failure. It keeps us from learning, from seeing our blind spots, and from adapting to new information. As we lean into overconfidence, we may find ourselves taking unnecessary risks, overlooking critical details, or doubling down on flawed strategies. The brain, seduced by its own narrative, drives us forward with the false conviction that we are in control, even as reality offers subtle signs to the contrary. By understanding these psychological processes, we can begin to unravel the intricate web of overconfidence, recognizing it not as a simple flaw, but as a complex, deeply ingrained aspect of our cognitive makeup—a trait that has the power to inspire great action, but also one that can lead us towards blind ambition.

Imagine Jason, a rising star in the investing industry. He is in his early thirties, the kind of person who quickly demands attention in meetings, his confidence evident as he discusses market prospects. Jason believed that his success was due to more than simply chance. He had made all of the correct decisions, investing in promising tech companies at precisely the right time, catching the wave before anybody else. Every move appeared to show him properly, and each victory fuelled his feeling of invincibility. His portfolio was not just expanding; it was flourishing, and his colleagues took note. Jason began to feel like he was finally in the game, really in it. He did not simply follow the market; he predicted it. He was ahead of the curve, detecting patterns that others did not and acting when others hesitated. He had completed three consecutive winning deals, and a euphoric surge of power accompanied his triumph. The financial markets resembled a turbulent sea, and Jason felt he had conquered the waves, riding them with accuracy and grace.

Then followed the announcement of a new electric car company. It was creating ripples, but only among those "in the know." Jason felt proud to be one of them. He recognised this firm as a hidden jewel, poised to revolutionise the automobile sector with unparalleled ingenuity and infinite potential. He could already envision it: getting in early, riding the wave while everyone else tried to catch up, and seeing his investment grow tenfold. He did not hesitate. He transferred practically everything—liquidated the safe, diversified his assets, and doubled down on one gamble. It was all or nothing, and he was sure that it would be everything. At first, Jason's instincts looked correct. The stock soared, and he saw the figures increase on his screen, confirming his genius. Articles in financial periodicals repeated his thoughts, and others began to notice. Jason grinned knowingly since he had seen it first. The pleasure of the early returns further strengthened his conviction—he was ahead of the pack, and he would soon enjoy the benefits of seeing the future before anybody else.

But then, the market shifted. Initially, there was almost no discernible change in mood. There were rumours of increasing interest rates and suggestions that growth stocks may not be as impregnable as everyone had thought. Jason rejected it. He had encountered critics before, and they had always been incorrect. He told himself that this was simply noise, that the volatility would pass. He understood the true significance of the situation, and he expected the market to recover. But the whispers became louder. Suddenly, the media that had previously hailed the electric car industry started to bring out flaws—production delays, increased competition, and cash flow concerns. Investors began to withdraw out, and Jason saw his once-soaring investment plummet. His screen, which had previously been green, now became a sea of crimson. He convinced himself it was simply a little setback. He persisted, sure that the price would return. After all, was not he correct?

Weeks passed, and the issue became worse. Jason felt himself caught, unwilling to sell since he trusted his judgement. He had ridden the highs, but now he was trapped in the lows, seeing the value diminish day after day. The same confidence that had propelled him to make risky decisions now bound him, closing his eyes to reality. He was losing more than just money; he was also losing the feeling of control he had fought so hard to develop. Jason had failed to understand that the market does not care about your beliefs. It does not encourage overconfidence or regard for the ego. It merely moves, oblivious to those who believe they have figured it out. Jason's success was genuine, but it was never the product of exceptional insight that others needed to gain. It required talent, timing, and a decent bit of luck. The confidence that had previously seemed like his greatest strength had now become his most significant vulnerability.

Overconfidence of Trading

Overconfidence is a subtle but enticing temptation. It seeps in with each success, hinting that you have outsmarted the market and have something that others do not. It seems powerful, but it is deceptive—it closes your eyes to hazards, prevents you from challenging your preconceptions, and convinces you that you are the exception. Jason's tale is not unusual. It is the narrative of innumerable investors, each of whom believes they have conquered the system before discovering the hard way that the market has a way of humiliating those who refuse to see their limitations.

Excessive trading is one of the most apparent indications of investor overconfidence. Investors who overestimate their ability to time the market tend to buy and sell often, thinking they can profit from even little price fluctuations. However, research shows that such vigorous trading usually produces lower returns than more cautious, passive systems. Barber and Odean (2000) discovered that those who traded the most actively had much lower net returns than those who traded less often. The explanation is simple: every transaction incurs related costs—brokerage fees, taxes, and bid-ask spreads—which eventually erode profits. Overconfident investors usually fail to account for these cumulative costs, assuming that their better decision-making would outweigh any fees spent. In practice, however, regular asset rebalancing seldom pays off, and attempting to "beat the market" typically results in underperformance.

Another aspect of overconfidence is the illusion of control, in which investors believe they can affect market outcomes. This perception often leads to a false feeling of security and increased vulnerability to danger. For example, an investor may think that their comprehensive study and expertise enable them to foresee future stock fluctuations correctly. This illusion is compounded by selective memory of earlier triumphs, in which investors remember successful investments while quickly forgetting losses. In the unpredictable and volatile world of financial markets, there are several elements outside any individual's control, ranging from macroeconomic swings to geopolitical developments (Petri, 2021). Believing that one can forecast or control these factors results in dangerous, concentrated holdings and a disregard for the advantages of portfolio diversification. The illusion of control inhibits investors from seeing the need to distribute risk across asset classes, which is a critical premise for managing uncertainty.

Overestimation of knowledge is another typical sign of overconfidence, in which investors believe they have better information compared to the general market. This assumption often leads to the dismissal of conflicting data or the failure to consider danger factors. Investors who feel they "know better" tend to depend excessively on limited information, believing that their perspectives are more informed than those of others. The risks of this bias are most apparent in market bubbles. During instances of enthusiasm, like the dot-com boom in the late 1990s, investors persuaded themselves that their knowledge of the technology industry enabled them to predict future winners, ignoring standard valuation measures. This overestimation of expertise may also result in confirmation bias, in which investors seek out information that confirms their previous views while rejecting any evidence that shows they may need to be corrected. This narrowing of focus may drive investors to remain too committed to positions that are no longer sustainable, resulting in lost opportunities and severe losses.

Underestimating danger is closely related to overestimating knowledge. Investors who are overconfident in their projections are more likely to feel they can weather downturns or avoid adverse outcomes, causing them to take on more risk than their circumstances warrant (Shefrin & Statman, 1985). Individual and institutional investors overestimated the dangers associated with mortgage-backed securities and collateralised debt obligations during the housing boom that preceded the 2008 Global Financial Crisis. The widespread perception was that increasing property values would continue forever, reducing the danger of subprime lending. This overconfidence in the market's stability encouraged excessive risk-taking, which culminated in devastating losses when the bubble burst. The financial crash demonstrated how deeply rooted overconfidence had become in market participants' behaviour, causing them to underestimate the likelihood and severity of unfavourable occurrences.

Overconfidence also has a significant influence on diversity, an essential part of risk management. Investors who are overconfident in their projections often need to diversify their holdings more appropriately. Instead of investing across numerous sectors or asset classes, they focus their assets in areas where they think they have better expertise. This concentration increases exposure to sector-specific risks, making the portfolio more sensitive to adverse developments in that market. For example, an investor may devote a significant amount of their portfolio to technology companies, assuming that their understanding of the industry would shield them against downturns. However, if the industry suffers an unforeseen setback—such as greater regulation or a technology shift—the investor's lack of diversification might result in significant losses. Overconfidence, in turn, adds to a failure to recognise the need to hedge against uncertainty, resulting in a portfolio that is less robust to market changes.

Another illustration of the consequences of overconfidence may be seen in the actions of institutional investors and fund managers. Regardless of their skill, fund managers are susceptible to the confidence trap. Many actively managed funds underperform their benchmark indexes, in part because fund managers believe they can reliably find booming equities. The active management paradox demonstrates that even expert investors, with access to substantial data and resources, fail to beat passive strategies over time. Overconfident managers may engage in frequent trading, take more significant risks, or need to adjust their approach to changing market circumstances, all of which may have a detrimental influence on fund performance. According to studies, actively managed funds need to catch up to passive index funds, especially after accounting for management fees and trading expenses. Overconfidence among professional investors, coupled with the drive to create short-term profits, often leads to judgements that harm long-term performance.

In the years running up to 2008, Wall Street was inundated with optimism. It was not apparent arrogance; instead, it was a quiet certainty, a deeply established sense that they had it all figured out. Mortgage-backed securities, or bundles of house loans that guaranteed returns with minimum risk, were the financial world's crown jewels. Banks and investors alike viewed them like gold, believing that their complex models and high credit ratings made them impenetrable. It was as if everyone on Wall Street had agreed that this was the new alchemy: transforming ordinary American mortgages into gems that could be endlessly exchanged for profit. Why would not they believe that? The gains were phenomenal, and as long as housing values rose, everyone profited.

The difficulty was that this notion was based on a shaky house of cards, with each level relying on unrealistic assumptions. Investors, hedge fund managers, and even senior executives were trapped in a self-created bubble, misled by their success and the attraction of easy money. They were confident that the diversification of these mortgage-backed securities—hundreds or thousands of house loans packaged together—would eliminate the underlying risk. It was a typical instance of overconfidence, exacerbated by complicated financial language and flashy AAA grades bestowed by credit agencies that seemed too anxious to keep the game running.

Wall Street's best thinkers thought they were smarter than everyone else. They invested billions of dollars in collateralised debt obligations (CDOs), believing that their knowledge of sophisticated risk models rendered them immune to market downturns. Risk managers, investment bankers, and traders all believed that diversifying subprime loans lowered risk to almost nothing. The fact that more and more loans were being made to those with poor credit records was seen as an opportunity. The more loans issued, the more they could package, slice, and sell. And each time they did, someone made a significant profit. It seemed to be a never-ending money machine powered by overconfidence.

Cracks were growing under the surface, however. The models that promised protection were predicated on the notion that property values would constantly rise—that the basis of American homeownership was stable and unshakeable. Investors were encouraged by prior success and overlooked the warning indicators that started to appear. Mortgage defaults began to rise, but many dismissed them as blips on the radar due to their overwhelming trust in the system. As long as the majority was confident and the ratings were high, there seemed to be no cause for concern. In their minds, they were not gambling; they were following a plan based on data, arithmetic, and the assumption that they understood more than anybody else.

When the bubble ultimately burst, the overconfidence faded into incredulity. Home values plummeted, mortgage defaults skyrocketed, and CDOs that had previously appeared like safe bets became toxic assets overnight. Banks that had put billions into these securities were now on the verge of failure. Lehman Brothers, formerly one of Wall Street's most renowned brands, declared bankruptcy with over $600 billion in assets, which were now worth a fraction of their stated value. Overconfidence has caused investors to disregard hazards and unquestioningly believe models and ratings, resulting in one of history's most disastrous financial disasters.

The overconfidence trap is a siren song in the world of investing—enticing, soothing, but ultimately dangerous. It leads investors to believe that they have mastered the complexity of financial markets and that their insights are infallible. That success is due to their superior talents rather than a combination of events and timing. It is a worldview that offers comfort by giving a sense of control in an inherently chaotic environment. However, as history has often shown, false confidence frequently leads to risk-taking, disregarding warning signals, and taking on more than one can actually manage. What makes overconfidence so hazardous is that it tends to reinforce itself. Each victory strengthens the assumption that you have it right, that your intuition is superior to the market's reality. It closes your eyes to the truth that the financial world is constantly changing, turbulent, and impacted by a plethora of forces beyond your comprehension. Overconfidence narrows your attention, ignoring the intricacies, unpredictability, and inherent hazards that accompany every financial choice.

Chapter 6

Overconfidence and Portfolio Mismanagement

Overconfidence is one of the most common behavioural biases among investors, often leading to poor portfolio management. Overconfidence, defined as an overestimation of one's talents or expertise, may present itself in a variety of ways during financial decision-making, notably in how investors manage their portfolios. Overconfidence bias has serious consequences, including excessive trading, under-diversification, risk misjudgment, and an unwillingness to modify tactics in reaction to changing market circumstances. Examining the impacts of overconfidence on portfolio management reveals that this cognitive bias not only influences decision-making processes but also presents a direct danger to the long-term viability of investment portfolios.

Excessive Trading

Excessive trading is one of the most common ways that overconfidence affects portfolio management. Consider an investor who views themselves as a market savant—someone who feels they can outperform the odds and recognise opportunities that others do not. They tell themselves that by timing their transactions perfectly, they may grab elusive short-term gains while generating steady profits. This overconfident mentality usually results in what is known as "excessive trading." Fuelled by an unyielding conviction in their expertise, these investors trade much more frequently than is prudent. Every time they click "buy" or "sell," they believe they are making the proper decision and think their market knowledge offers them an advantage. However, multiple studies have shown that excessive trading does not result in higher returns—in fact, it often leads to poorer results. Investors who traded frequently regularly underperformed those who followed a buy-and-hold approach. The frequent buying and selling generate a pile of expenses, including booking fees, taxes, and the bid-ask spread, all of which gradually eat away at portfolio gains. And that is not even getting into the behavioural pitfalls—overconfident investors are renowned for making terrible timing choices. They purchase when prices are high, motivated by optimism, and sell when prices fall, driven by fear—a strategy that is absolutely unhelpful to wealth growth. What begins as a confident chase of profits often devolved into a never-ending cycle of chasing losses, with nothing to show except reduced returns.

Another negative consequence of overconfidence is under-diversification. Diversification is a critical component of sound risk management—spreading assets across asset classes, industries, and regions to mitigate volatility. However, overconfident investors view things differently. They persuade themselves that they can choose a few profitable stocks, wagering that their picks would outperform the market. This approach results in a concentrated portfolio, with a few selected assets comprising the bulk of their holdings. Such concentration exposes the investor to high idiosyncratic risk—risks associated with particular firms or sectors that, if not managed properly, might result in catastrophic losses. Imagine an investor who is overconfident in their knowledge of the technology industry. They may devote a significant amount of their portfolio to technology companies, thinking that their experience gives them an advantage. However, the IT industry, like all others, is susceptible to downturns. Regulatory changes, competition, and economic changes might all contribute to a sector-wide downturn. If the investor has not diversified, they are susceptible, with little protections in place to mitigate the damage. When the risks are underestimated, what seemed to be a well-planned portfolio soon becomes a risky bet.

Overconfidence often blinds investors to the need for resilience. Instead of acknowledging that the future is unpredictable and that no one can precisely foresee market movements, overconfident people believe they have everything figured out. They reject diversity as a defensive strategy for less capable people, failing to see that even the most robust investing ideas have risks that can only be minimised by adequate diversification. Overreliance on stock-picking—believing that a few well-picked stocks can generate outsized returns—exposes the portfolio to massive volatility. The risk is not simply one stock underperforming; it is a more significant occurrence that might affect a whole industry or asset class. Without a safety net of various assets, investors are vulnerable to shocks that may have been mitigated or even avoided with a balanced strategy.

Overconfidence is ironic since it masquerades as a strength. It leads investors to assume they have a distinct advantage, resulting in frequent transactions and undiversified portfolios. However, it is their confidence that ultimately leads them astray, causing them to neglect the fundamentals of excellent investing strategy. Markets are inherently unpredictable, and making aggressive bets is not always the best strategy. It is often about having the humility to admit what you do not know and the discipline to prepare for the unexpected. Overconfident investors may not see it at first, but their pursuit of market outperformance is really stacking the deck against them. The prices build-up, the dangers grow, and what began as a confident strategy to outperform the market quickly becomes a sharp lesson in the value of moderation and diversity.

Overconfidence may substantially affect how investors estimate risk, causing them to take on too much exposure without fully understanding the possible drawbacks. Consider an investor who feels they are invincible—that they have a unique power to influence the results of their investments. This mindset often drives people to employ leverage, a solid but hazardous tactic that entails borrowing money to increase their investment. The argument appears straightforward: double your investment doubles your profits. But what is sometimes overlooked is that leverage works both ways—it magnifies losses. Overconfident investors believe that their superior knowledge and abilities will keep them safe. In fact, turbulent markets may transform a seemingly winning wager into a losing one overnight. Leveraged positions may collapse swiftly, prompting margin calls that drive investors to sell assets at rock-bottom prices only to satisfy their loans. This avalanche of selling may quickly wipe out a portfolio, leaving once-confident investors wondering what went wrong. In reality, the most significant error was underestimating risk in the first place, assuming that success was particular just because they felt they knew better.

Overconfidence also has a negative impact on adaptability. Investors often cling to their early strategy, even when the situation changes substantially. This rigidity is fuelled in part by confirmation bias, a cognitive trap in which people seek out information that confirms their pre-existing opinions while rejecting anything that contradicts them. This prejudice is common among overconfident investors. Consider an investor who buys shares in a firm because they believe it is the next great thing. Even when signals of trouble surface, such as deteriorating profitability, litigation, or new rivals, the overconfident investor deliberately ignores these warning signs. They concentrate only on the positive news, reaffirming their initial choice while disregarding the fissures growing under the surface. Their unwillingness to rethink their approach and confront the facts means they are holding onto a sinking ship, which not only affects that single stock but may also drag down their whole portfolio. The refusal to alter course in the face of solid evidence that it is time to do so is a defining feature of how overconfidence may lead to poor portfolio management.

The illusion of control, or the erroneous belief that one can affect or forecast the market more than one can, is a significant cause of overconfidence. This tendency leads investors to make judgements based on the notion that they have unique insight, which is typically linked to their own experiences or expertise. Consider an investor who works in the pharmaceutical sector. They believe that their industry expertise offers them an advantage when deciding which pharmaceutical companies to purchase. And, although insider knowledge might aid in understanding the complexities of a business, it does not guarantee insulation from more considerable market hazards. Regulatory changes or economic downturns may influence even the most promising enterprises, and this investor's belief in their ability to control the result might drive them to overinvest in one industry. They may believe that diversity is unnecessary because they "know better," but no amount of knowledge can forecast a regulatory shift or an unexpected new competition. The appearance of control breeds misguided confidence, leading to portfolios concentrated on sectors that are particularly susceptible to abrupt and unforeseen shocks.

Overconfidence is very closely related to another cognitive bias: anchoring. This is the inclination to focus on previous experiences and believe that what worked previously would work again, regardless of present circumstances. Investors who rely on past triumphs sometimes need help to adjust when market conditions change. Consider someone who amassed a fortune by investing significantly in growth stocks during a bull market. They begin to assume that they have the golden touch and that these companies would always generate large profits. When the market turns towards value investing or more stable assets, they continue to pump money into growth companies, believing that previous performance ensures future benefits. However, markets fluctuate, and techniques that work well in one economic situation may fail in another. Anchoring in prior successes, fuelled by overconfidence that history will repeat itself, results in portfolios that need to be aligned with current reality, exposing investors to needless risks or allowing them to lose out on more attractive prospects.

Overconfidence Trap

The overconfidence trap is one of the most deceiving investment fallacies. It disguises itself as decisiveness and certainty, qualities that many people value, particularly in the high-stakes world of banking. However, underneath the façade of self-assurance, overconfidence often conceals a reluctance to accept reality—whether it is the truth of market volatility, the limitations of one's power, or the need to change strategy when the winds shift. Investors who fall into this trap end up with portfolios that are excessively risky, insufficiently diversified, and sensitive to unexpected shocks. To escape this destiny, humility is essential. Accepting that no one, not even the most successful, experienced investor, can control or foresee every event is the first step towards risk management and creating a portfolio that can withstand both good and bad times.

Overconfidence also causes a reluctance to seek outside counsel or examine different perspectives, which may be damaging to portfolio management. Investors who are confident in their talents often assume that they do not need assistance or second views, especially while navigating complicated markets or making high-risk selections. This may lead to insular thinking, in which investors are more susceptible to confirmation bias and less willing to question their ideas. Overconfident investors lose crucial insights by neglecting to engage others or explore other viewpoints, which might help them discover weaknesses in their portfolio plan or better appreciate the risks they are incurring. Overconfidence is characterised by a failure to enjoy the benefits of external expertise, which often leads to severe investment mismanagement.

The idea of "over-precision" is equally important in portfolio management. Over-precision is an investor's unfounded conviction that they have an exact forecast of future market movements or specific asset performance. This assumption might lead to unduly restricted expectations about the likely outcomes of their investments, leading to insufficient planning for unfavourable situations. For example, an investor may be so convinced that a given stock would increase by a certain percentage within a specified period that they neglect to examine the range of possible outcomes, including the possibility of adverse events affecting the company's performance. This failure to explore alternate options exposes the portfolio to unforeseen market shocks since the investor needs to hedge against prospective risks appropriately.

This is an illustration of how overconfidence may have disastrous implications for an investment. Emma Caldwell was unstoppable. Every morning, she stepped into her glass-walled office on the 34th floor of her Manhattan skyscraper, and her presence was magnetic. She was the star analyst everyone aspired to be. She talked in soundbites that were often cited in business periodicals, and her forecasts were generally correct. Emma exuded a calm assurance to her coworkers, making even the most nervous market days seem like just another Friday.

In 2021, the globe was recovering from the pandemic's havoc. Markets that had previously been on the verge of collapse were surging back into life. Emma saw an opportunity—a golden wave ready to be ridden. She had created a name for herself by anticipating the development of technology during the pandemic's deadliest days, tripling her customers' portfolios and establishing a reputation as a bold innovator. However, there was something fresh on the horizon. Clean energy was no longer a buzzword; it represented the future. The news was full of electric car businesses and solar energy advancements, and Emma knew she needed to get in early. SolarNova was one of these emerging stars, with ambitious plans to change the solar panel industry. Emma was mesmerised. The creator was a charismatic former engineer with a track record that suggested grandeur, and the promise of SolarNova's groundbreaking technology was alluring. Emma was confident she had discovered the next big thing—her own Apple or Tesla moment. She gambled big, investing millions of her customers' funds in the business. Diversification? That was for people who were unable to see the future as clearly as she could. Emma was all in and was going to win.

At first, it seemed magical. SolarNova shares surged when the firm went public. Emma's instincts looked immaculate once again. Her customers saw their net worth increase, and their trust in her was unwavering. The exhilaration was palpable, a heady combination of accomplishment and affirmation. They celebrated their riches in rooftop parties, and Emma basked in their adulation, champagne glass lifted high. She saw this as her brilliance at work—her unique capacity to perceive what others could not. It was the kind of assurance that made her feel unstoppable. But under the surface, SolarNova was collapsing. Delays and soaring manufacturing costs beset their ambitious deployment. The murmurs of alarm started slowly among business insiders, and Emma disregarded them as mere noise. After all, she had seen the founder and witnessed the spark of ambition in his eyes, which was plenty for her. But the market was not as readily persuaded. The quarterly profits report was released, and it was a catastrophe. Revenues were falling short, estimates were lowered, and the dream began to shatter.

Emma studied the data on her screen with surprise as SolarNova's stock plummeted. Her clientele, who had previously toasted to her genius, were now ringing in terror. Their portfolios were losing value right in front of her eyes. Emma maintained her belief, telling herself that this was just temporary. She had been right before, and she would be right again. This time, however, things were different. The losses continued to build, and eventually, margin calls forced her hand, compelling her to liquidate assets at a fraction of their worth in order to fund her leveraged gamble. What began as a tale of brilliance evolved into a bitter lesson in arrogance. Emma mistook her previous accomplishments for infallibility. She had convinced herself that she was unique—that the market could be twisted to her will. Now, as she sat in her office late at night, staring at the deserted skyline, she realised her actual error. She had misjudged not just SolarNova but also herself. The hazards she would disregard, the cautions she would discount, everything came flooding back, and for the first time in years, Emma felt small—just another investor who had made a mistake.

Emma Caldwell's story is not unusual, but it is very human. It tells the narrative of how overconfidence may cause even the most gifted investors to lose sight of the fundamentals—to forget that the market is unpredictable, that diversity is a safety net, and that no one, not even the brightest star, can see everything clearly. The lesson from Emma's failure is more than simply a squandered investment. It is about the fine line between confidence and arrogance and how, in the enticing heat of success, it is all too easy to forget that the market owes you nothing. In the end, the market's harsh truth reminds even the greatest among us that humility is the only way to win in the long term genuinely.

The cumulative impact of these overconfident behaviours—excessive trading, under-diversification, risk misjudgment, inability to evaluate strategies, the illusion of control, anchoring, unwillingness to seek external counsel, and over-precision—leads to considerable portfolio mismanagement. Overconfident investors, who overestimate their capacity to forecast and influence market events, often take on more risk than they can manage, engage in poorly timed transactions, and hang onto assets that are beyond their prime. These behaviours not only reduce possible profits but also expose the portfolio to increased risk, raising the possibility of significant financial losses.

A more thorough examination of the psychological and cognitive elements that contribute to overconfidence will help us better understand this complicated and widespread behavioural bias, which impacts investors of all skill levels. Validation bias, which happens when people ignore contradicting data in favour of information that supports their preexisting opinions or decisions, is a substantial cognitive bias that is linked to overconfidence. By ignoring important evidence that contradicts their presumptions and favouring information that confirms their previous beliefs, this bias feeds the overconfident investor's propensity to believe in their own skills. This gives individuals a false sense of security and causes them to base their decisions on incomplete or erroneous knowledge, which exacerbates the detrimental impacts of overconfidence.

Another psychological factor that supports overconfidence in investing is the Dunning-Kruger effect. This cognitive bias refers to the propensity of people who have little experience or expertise in a given field to overestimate their own competence in that field. When it comes to investing, inexperienced or inexperienced individuals may have unrealistic expectations about their capacity to forecast market trends or choose profitable stocks. They frequently take on excessive risks as a result of their exaggerated self-perception, thinking they have better market knowledge than they actually do, even when they lack the expertise to make wise choices. Thus, the Dunning-Kruger effect exacerbates overconfidence, increasing the chance of serious portfolio mismanagement and putting people at greater risk of making poor decisions.

Together with overconfidence, these biases produce a risky cycle in which the investor's overconfidence in their skills causes them to become oblivious to their knowledge gaps and the inherent uncertainties of the market. This emphasizes how crucial it is to remain humble and look for many viewpoints in order to combat the distortions brought on by arrogance. Investors can better manage their portfolios and steer clear of the dangers of taking on too much risk and making bad decisions by being aware of and addressing these cognitive biases.

Chapter 7

The Emotional Rollercoaster:
Overreaction and Market Anomalies

Consider standing in the centre of a packed amusement park, with the sounds of funfair games and the aroma of popcorn filling the air. Ahead of you lies the rollercoaster, with its twisting rails disappearing into the sky. When navigating financial markets, investors are often trapped between the pleasure of the ride and the dread of the impending plummet. The markets, like that rollercoaster, may excite, frighten, and confound all at once. Investors, despite their claims to be calm and reasonable, are often just along for the ride, affected by every twist and turn. This is the domain of overreaction and market oddities, where emotions converge with decision-making, and logic often takes a second seat.

Overreaction

The notion of overreaction is not new. It is something we witness in our daily lives: how individuals exaggerate the significance of a slight annoyance or get ecstatic about a modest accomplishment. However, in the financial sector, overreaction may have far-reaching implications. Consider a corporation that reports a brief decline in profits. Perhaps they missed a profit goal by a few pennies, or their quarterly forecast could have been more optimistic. In a perfect environment, investors would examine the situation, evaluate the fundamentals, and alter their holdings as needed. Instead, terror sets in. Traders push the sell button, and the stock price plummets—sometimes losing a third or even half of its worth within hours. Investors begin to feel that this tiny setback is a symptom of far more significant problems, and the frenzy feeds on itself. The downturn snowballs into a collapse, not because the firm is inherently weak but because the market as a whole lost its calm.

Conversely, overreaction does not necessarily lead to a panic sell-off. Sometimes, the markets are overcome with enthusiasm. Take the biotechnology industry, for example. A business reports early data that indicate promise in an experimental therapy. Investors rush to acquire shares, driving up values to ludicrous heights. Analysts hop on board, financial television networks run headlines with phrases like "revolutionary" and "game-changer," and individual investors, desperate not to fall behind, deposit their funds in the company. But the fact is that there are still years of testing, regulatory difficulties, and uncertainty ahead. While the news is thrilling, it does not support a sudden increase in the company's market value. However, this level of enthusiasm is indicative of overreaction. Investors get engrossed in the fantasy, and reality takes a back place to the fiction being delivered.

Overreaction in financial markets is firmly ingrained in human psychology, formed by cognitive constraints that influence our decision-making processes. Overreaction is mainly caused by emotional biases and mental shortcuts known as heuristics, which are designed to simplify complicated judgements (De Bondt & Thaler, 1985). Investors cannot constantly evaluate every piece of information logically; instead, they depend on intuitive impulses that are often affected by fear, greed, and overconfidence. These emotional drives may exaggerate reactions to market news, causing price swings that significantly outweigh the actual relevance of the information. For example, negative news may induce a far more significant sell-off than necessary since the agony of possible losses often overcomes the reasonable assessment of long-term possibilities. The psychological impulse to "avoid regret" drives investors to behave rashly, resulting in a domino effect of overreaction that impacts the whole market.

People tend to perceive gains and losses in an imbalanced manner—losses seem more acute than comparable gains. In financial markets, this often implies that bad news elicits a more significant response than favourable news, causing investors to make emotional rather than sensible choices. When confronted with the threat of a loss, many investors tend to behave defensively, quickly selling up their assets to prevent future losses. This impulse to protect oneself from losses may lead to severe market sell-offs, even when a more prudent option would be to remain stable. The weight of possible losses influences investor behaviour, resulting in overreactions that may misalign prices, at least briefly. Such responses are not limited to individuals; they may have global ripple effects, as one person's panic-driven selling pushes others to do the same, hence increasing volatility and exacerbating market downturns.

The availability heuristic also has a substantial impact on overreaction. This cognitive bias refers to people's propensity to judge the probability of an occurrence depending on how readily examples spring to mind. When investors are bombarded with news about a company's failing performance, the vividness and recurrence of that news become the most accessible information in their brains. This causes an overemphasis on recent unfavourable occurrences, and investors may overreact, selling off shares despite the company's more significant, long-term prospects. Essentially, the brain employs a mental shortcut to assess danger swiftly, but it often overestimates the importance of recent occurrences. This sort of overreaction is focused on the salience of information rather than its fundamental importance to the company's prospects.

Overreaction, according to sociology, is about more than simply individual biases; it is also about collective behaviour and social impact dynamics. Investors often base their judgements on the behaviour of others, particularly in uncertain circumstances. Sociologists call this "social proof," in which individuals believe that the acts of others represent proper behaviour. When a significant investor or a considerable number of market participants respond strongly to an incident, it might set off a chain reaction, causing others to follow suit. This propensity is exacerbated by media coverage, which magnifies reports of significant market fluctuations and supports the belief that if everyone else is responding in the same manner, it must be the reasonable thing to do. As a consequence of this herd behaviour, prices might diverge significantly from their underlying values.

Emotional Contagion

Emotional contagion is another social idea that leads to market overreaction. Emotional contagion is the mechanism by which emotions spread between individuals, similar to how infections spread. Fear or enthusiasm in the financial markets may spread quickly. When a renowned investor sells a significant investment out of fear, it causes alarm among others, prompting them to follow suit. The collective emotional response builds, resulting in an overreaction that may transform a seemingly sensible move into a market-wide panic. This is why market collapses are often defined not just by individual irrationality but also by a communal plunge into fear-driven decision-making (Shiller, 2000). Emotional contagion may cause a feedback loop in which emotions magnify one another, resulting in movements that are entirely divorced from the underlying economic fundamentals.

The sociology of overreaction includes the notion of social conformance. Even experienced and sensible investors may feel forced to conform to popular opinion. The fear of standing alone, of being viewed as missing something that others notice, might lead investors to forego their research in favour of crowdsourcing. This propensity to conform is powerful during times of uncertainty when making autonomous judgements seems riskier than just following the herd. Because of this conformity, tiny movements in response to news or events may be exacerbated as more investors participate, resulting in large-scale overreactions that push markets away from equilibrium.

Market anomalies are the twists and turns in this emotional rollercoaster—unusual, repeating patterns that contradict conventional explanations. These oddities are typically the result of collective investor psychology. Market anomalies are those weird little interruptions that remind you that financial markets are not as perfect as they profess to be. Consider them as unanticipated wrinkles in a well-fitted suit—imperfections that break the flawless veneer of market efficiency. According to the traditional view, financial markets function like well-oiled machines, with prices reflecting every piece of available information, leaving no room for "easy money." However, anomalies emerge—those unpredictable blips where things do not behave as expected, where logic bends, and patterns emerge from seemingly nowhere. They are the moments that remind us that, despite the numerical calculations and complex models, markets are still made up of fallible, emotional, and occasionally illogical individuals.

These market oddities are what keep the financial world so interesting. They are like whispers in the unrest, little secrets that hint at something deeper under the surface. They debunk the myth that markets are completely efficient and that prices constantly move with perfect accuracy. Instead, they demonstrate that markets may be unpredictable and volatile, influenced by the same emotions, anxieties, and urges that individuals experience in their daily lives. Market anomalies demonstrate that, no matter how modern our technology or how precise our research is, the financial world is inherently unpredictable. They illustrate that human behaviour drives the market, with all of its imperfections and unforeseen twists.

Some investors see these abnormalities as a puzzle to be solved. Others see them as opportunities—moments to take advantage of when market inefficiencies provide profit potential. In the ever-changing financial world, anomalies serve as little windows into the truth that every transaction is a human choice influenced by biases and emotions. They highlight the contrast between the theoretical world of finance, in which everything is logical and efficient, and the actual world, in which things do not always make perfect sense. These idiosyncrasies call into question the notion that markets are well-ordered, efficient entities, pointing instead to the underlying complexity—the intertwined variables of psychology, attitude, and behaviour that bring markets to life.

What makes market oddities so appealing is their unpredictability. They are similar to wild cards in a deck—sometimes disruptive, often unexpected, and always a reminder that financial markets are more than just equations and data points. They represent the complex dance between data-driven reasoning and the emotional heartbeats of investors throughout the globe. These anomalies highlight the contradiction between tidy, ordered financial theories and the chaotic, unpredictable character of human behaviour. And it is in this zone, between order and chaos, that the most exciting chances emerge. They encourage investors to delve beyond established models, probe more profound, and question assumptions.

One of the most well-known is the January Effect, which occurs when stock values, especially those of smaller businesses, perform better in January than any other month. The financial industry has proposed several hypotheses to explain this pattern: maybe it is driven by investors purchasing back equities they sold for tax purposes in December, or perhaps it reflects the excitement that comes with a new year. Whatever the origin, the January Effect endures, serving as a reminder that markets are more than cold, efficient mechanisms— they are highly human, influenced by the attitudes and behaviours of individuals who participate.

Consider the Monday Effect, which shows that stock returns are lower on Mondays than on other days of the week. There is no economic rule that states Mondays should be worse for the markets than Wednesdays or Fridays, yet this oddity has been seen for decades. Some relate it to investors' propensity to analyse negative news over the weekend, resulting in a "sell" feeling on Monday morning. Others argue that it is merely a self-fulfilling prophecy: investors anticipate Mondays will be worse, so they take actions that lead prices to fall. It is a modest but revealing illustration of how investor psychology influences the market in subtle but significant ways.

Overreaction is directly related to our fundamental biases—fear, greed, and the constant need for clarity in an unpredictable environment. Fear, of course, is one of the most potent motivators. When panic grips the market, reason goes out the window. During the 2008 financial crisis, investors sold everything they could—stocks, bonds, even gold—in a desperate attempt to convert their assets into cash, the ultimate safety net. In retrospect, this response caused more damage than good, locking in losses at precisely the wrong moment. The sell-off was fuelled not by a reasoned assessment of each investment's worth but by a visceral, communal terror that set off a downward cycle.

Greed, on the other hand, causes us to make hasty judgements during market booms. When everything seems to be going up, we might easily persuade ourselves that the celebration will never stop. This kind of overreaction causes investors to pump money into assets they hardly comprehend just because everyone else is doing it. The dot-com bubble is a perfect example: in the late 1990s, firms with nothing more than a concept for a website were valued in the billions. Investors could not acquire enough shares, and even seasoned professionals were caught up in the thrill of the "new economy." The rush to get in, combined with the collective dread of losing out, fuelled a bubble that was doomed to pop.

It is interesting how rapidly investor mood can shift. One day, a corporation is seen as the darling of Wall Street, the next as the devil. These emotional fluctuations are not caused by actual company operations or underlying value; instead, they are caused by perception, self-talk, and assumptions about what others are thinking. This fosters a climate in which anomalies—unexpected, illogical market behaviours—can flourish. Another well-documented phenomenon is the Momentum Effect, which states that companies that have done well in the past are likely to perform well in the near term. At the same time, those that have underperformed continue to lag. This is caused by the herd mentality, in which investors follow recent winners, sure that the momentum will continue, while selling losers are frightened of additional drops. As a consequence, prices deviate more from their inherent value due to a feedback loop.

There is also the "flight to quality" phenomenon, which occurs when investors transfer in large numbers from hazardous assets to safe ones during a crisis. This behaviour was evident during the COVID-19 epidemic, when, confronted with global uncertainty, investors sold equities in favour of government bonds, pushing rates to record lows. It was not that every enterprise had suddenly become worthless; instead, investors were overcome with panic. The rush to find safety caused a momentary distortion in the market, highlighting the emotional aspect of investment during tumultuous times. It demonstrates how the same overreaction that creates asset bubbles in good times can result in indiscriminate sell-offs in poor times.

Overconfidence and Market Anomalies

One especially intriguing feature of overreaction is how it impacts experienced investors who have seen market cycles come and go. During the 2008 financial crisis, even the most skilled fund managers overreacted. The quick sell-off of mortgage-backed securities, for example, was fuelled not just by data but also by a communal realisation—almost a social panic—that these products were riskier than anybody had anticipated. When panic sets in, even people with the most significant information at their disposal struggle to stay impartial; it is a poignant reminder that markets are fundamentally made up of innately emotional people.

Market oddities such as the small-cap premium—the propensity for smaller firms to outperform bigger ones over time—demonstrate the peculiar ways in which overreaction and underreaction coexist. When small businesses outperform, it is frequently due to their more significant growth potential. However, their outperformance is partly due to risk and the market's variable evaluation of that risk. During weak markets, small-cap equities suffer disproportionately as investors rush to more prominent, more reliable corporations. Then, during recoveries, these tiny businesses bounce back, often even overcorrecting, resulting in outsized profits. The market is constantly in motion and attempts to reach stability, so the rollercoaster ride continues.

Overreaction is also seen in the market's reaction to earnings shocks. When a firm outperforms expectations, its stock typically skyrockets, fuelled by enthusiasm and hope. When it misses, the penalty is fast and severe. However, an earnings beat or miss is frequently just a snapshot of a single quarter. It does not substantially alter the company's long-term course. Nonetheless, the market sees these occurrences as enormous, with prices moving considerably more than they should based on a single data point. It is an overreaction caused by our desire to simplify complicated information, labelling a firm as a winner or a loss based on insufficient data.

The "Halloween Effect" seems like something from a scary novel. As if the stock market takes on a secret personality, reacting to the changing seasons with uncanny precision. "Sell in May and go away, but remember to come back in November" is a phrase you may hear muttered among old-timers on Wall Street, an adage that seems more like superstition than financial advice. Nonetheless, this apparently folkloric knowledge has proved to be one of the most exciting and long-lasting market oddities, reappearing like a ghost every year to haunt standard financial ideas.

Imagine you are an investor, and the market consistently underperforms over the summer, only to surge dramatically from November to April. It is almost as if the market takes a vacation over the summer when traders are more interested in relaxing on the beach than trading equities. However, by November, things begin to pick up again. The brisk fall air welcomes traders back into their desks, and the market resumes its buzz—holiday sales estimates, renewed confidence, and a feeling of new possibility pervade the financial milieu. It is no coincidence, they claim. The evidence is there: traditionally, the months of November through April have outperformed the summer months, as if investors are intuitively matching their activities with the natural rhythm of the seasons.

The question is: Why? What is it about May that drives investors away, and what about the autumn that entices them back? Some argue it is a practical thing—summer is calmer, volumes are lower, and volatility rises. It is a time when Wall Street vacations trump investing choices, and the market suffers as a consequence. In contrast, the end of the year brings heightened market activity, with major institutional investors returning, economic data arriving, and corporations publishing profit estimates. There is a buzz of activity, a sense of hurry to get things done before the calendar reset. As consumers pack the malls and companies close their fiscal years, investors return, ready to be part of the activity.

However, it is more than simply trading volumes and business profitability; it is also about mood. It is about psychology. As the days shorten and the weather cools, people's behaviours shift, and the market seems to adapt. With the holidays approaching, there is a fresh air of excitement and expectation as corporations put out their big plans for the following year. Investors buy into the optimism—literally—and the market often rises on the tide of optimistic mood. The Halloween Effect is more than simply a calendar quirk; it reflects the optimism and cyclical energy that appears to increase as the end of the year approaches. It is as if the stock market senses the enthusiasm of the holidays and reacts accordingly.

Then there is the excitement of the hunt—the oddity has evolved into an opportunity that some investors actively pursue. They attempt to scam the system by selling in May to escape the quiet months and then jumping back in to catch the winter surge. But here is where things get really interesting: as more people believe in the Halloween Effect, it becomes a self-fulfilling prophecy. The action of selling in May and purchasing in November may, in turn, produce the pattern it seeks to exploit. It is a market enigma that defies simple explanation—one that lies at the crossroads of data, human behaviour, and, maybe, a little magic.

The Halloween Effect demonstrates how intricate and intriguing the financial markets are. Under the spreadsheets and data, there are patterns—some reasonable, others unexplained. No crystal ball can explain why November is better than June or why investors prefer to make significant investments in the winter rather than the summer. What we do know is that even in the most logical, numbers-driven areas of finance, human behaviour leaves its imprint. The market is more than just statistics and charts; it is people with all of their habits, hopes, and, yes, seasonal patterns. That is what distinguishes the Halloween Effect as more than simply a market strategy—it is a tale about how we live, the cycles we follow, and how, even in the realm of money, we are seasonal beings.

Asian financial markets are dynamic, complicated venues where local culture, investor psychology, and global economic factors mix, resulting in distinct, almost rhythmic patterns that captivate and perplex experts worldwide. These markets do not simply reflect Western models; rather, they exhibit particular impacts driven by long-held traditions, seasonal cycles, and communal attitudes. Let us take a look at the psychological and seasonal trends seen in Asia, from the January Effect to the intense, emotionally charged Flight to Quality in times of crisis. These occurrences are more than simply numerical anomalies; they are tales woven from human psychology and regional conventions, giving Asian markets an exceptional case study in behavioural finance.

In the heart of Japan's busy financial metropolis, the January Effect takes on cultural overtones, reflecting both a tax strategy and a cultural belief in new beginnings. This phenomenon, in which smaller firms see a boost in value at the start of the year, may be linked to more than simply investors returning from vacation. For Japanese investors, January is a culturally significant month, an almost holy chance to start over, reset financial objectives, and embrace the possibilities of the next year. The rush to repurchase equities sold in December to avoid capital gains taxes is undoubtedly a component, but there is also an undertone of confidence that feeds into the stock market, much like a New Year's resolve emerging on trading floors. Small-cap companies, which are frequently seen as riskier but potentially promise strong growth, are warmly welcomed back into portfolios. This optimism-fuelled purchasing rush converts January into a month of extraordinary profits, particularly for smaller, growth-oriented businesses. While the January Effect is also seen in Western markets, it is not only about money in Japan—it is about a cultural acceptance of a clean slate, a strong combination of budgetary practicality and emotional rejuvenation.

Moving south to Hong Kong, the Monday Effect takes on a new dimension. The universally observed habit of weaker market returns on Mondays takes on a new dimension here. Hong Kong is a bridge between East and West, and its physical and cultural location means that worldwide news, particularly from the United States, has a big impact. With Wall Street shutting late on Friday in relation to Hong Kong's time zone, any negative news has the whole weekend to penetrate investor mood in Hong Kong. By Monday, worry had grown, and traders approached the market with caution, if not pessimism. It is almost as if Hong Kong investors hold their breath during the weekend, preparing for the effect of Wall Street, and then let out a collective sigh—often in the form of a sell-off—on Monday morning. This increased Monday sensitivity is not an official regulation, but rather a legacy of market opinion formed by global interconnection. What was the result? Lower Monday returns have become a self-fulfilling prophesy, with traders expecting and creating them, repeating a decades-long trend.

Then there is the Lunar New Year Effect in China, Taiwan, and South Korea, which combines cultural tradition with financial behaviour in a manner that few other market trends do. The Lunar New Year is more than simply a holiday; it is a celebration of family, rejuvenation, and wealth, and it has a significant impact on these areas' financial markets each year. In the days preceding up to the holiday, investors often sell shares to turn them into cash, a practice that stems from the preparation of red envelopes—monetary presents for family and friends. As a consequence, the markets experience a momentary drop, a pre-celebration slump. However, something extraordinary occurs after the celebrations. The markets undergo a rebirth of sorts, as investors return with newfound hope, spurred by the traditional notion that the new lunar year offers new prospects and luck. This post-holiday surge has the appearance of a spring bloom in the financial markets, fuelled by a combination of cultural optimism and freshly accessible cash. The Lunar New Year Effect demonstrates how deeply financial markets may be knitted into the fabric of cultural identity—a reminder that in Asia, even money follows tradition.

However, when a crisis occurs, Asia, like other areas, displays another side of its financial psychology, with trends such as the Flight to Quality taking the front stage. The COVID-19 epidemic was an obvious illustration of this. As instances grew globally, investors from Tokyo to Jakarta started abandoning riskier assets in favour of government bonds, cash, and other "safe" investments. Despite Japan's traditionally low government bond rates, investors flocked to acquire them. Why? Because in times of severe uncertainty, it is not about the return; it is about knowing that the primary is safe. In Hong Kong, the Flight to Quality took on a geopolitical dimension, with investors shifting assets to the US dollar, fearing not just pandemic-driven market volatility but also regional political concerns. This mass exodus to safety is more than a tactical retreat; it is a very human reaction to fear, a representation of the impulse to seek refuge amid a storm. The Flight to Quality is not about optimism or strategy; it is about survival, a retreat to financial fortresses when difficult times arise.

Another noteworthy trend is the Momentum Effect, which has emerged in China and South Korea, particularly among retail investors, who now account for a significant amount of trading activity. In many nations, the importance of social networks, family guidance, and online forums fosters a climate in which momentum may grow quickly and effectively. Take, for example, the emergence of Chinese internet behemoths Tencent and Alibaba. When these companies started to perform well, ordinary investors flooded in, frequently encouraged by friends, family, or online groups, generating momentum that pushed prices even higher. It is a herd mentality-fuelled feedback loop: as more people purchase, prices climb, drawing even more buyers, all certain that the momentum will continue. In South Korea, the tendency is also evident in industries like as biotech and technology, where speculative purchases by retail investors often reflect societal emotion rather than financial realities. The Momentum Effect is both a social movement and an investing trend, a collective drive in which success is defined by riding the wave rather than comprehending the fundamentals. And, ultimately, as the momentum fades, the collapse may be just as quick, leaving a trail of retail investors who rode the high only to get caught in the final fall.

The price of Bitcoin skyrocketed from roughly $1,000 in January 2017 to almost $20,000 by December 2017 before plummeting to less than $4,000 in early 2018 during the 2017–2018 Bitcoin boom. Similar price movements took place between 2020 and 2021, as institutional adoption and retail speculation propelled Bitcoin's rise from over $10,000 in October 2020 to over $60,000 by March 2021. Bitcoin's tremendous volatility at these times reflects the market's overreaction, as investor fervour drove the price to unsupportable heights before a steep decline, illustrating the effects of fear and overconfidence.

The VIX (Volatility Index) also amply demonstrated the market's concern during the 2008 financial crisis. The VIX typically ranges from 10 to 20, but in October 2008, it reached over 80, indicating a severe case of panic. The overreaction fuelled by fear and herd mentality was exposed by this dramatic increase in the VIX. The crisis was made worse by the massive market disruptions brought on by panic-induced selling. The VIX spike demonstrated how emotional biases may lead to significant market price movements that go well beyond the true economic fundamentals.

Another well-known instance of market overreaction was the January 2021 GameStop episode. Retail investors on social media sites like Reddit were the main force behind the "short squeeze," which caused the price of GameStop stock to jump from around $20 at the start of January to an intraday high of $483 on January 28, 2021. Simultaneously, GameStop's short interest rate surpassed 140%, leaving the stock open to a short squeeze and contributing to the price volatility. With the market being driven by collective anxiety and the desire for riches, the enormous increase in retail trading volume demonstrated the strength of emotional contagion and herd behaviour. In addition to demonstrating overreaction to the stock, this incident demonstrated how investors' emotional reactions to "information overload" fuelled illogical price fluctuations.

Overreaction can also be understood theoretically according to the experimental data from Kahneman and Tversky's Prospect Theory. Their research revealed a phenomenon called loss aversion, which occurs when people see losses more negatively than comparable gains. This idea explains why investors tend to react more strongly to negative news than to positive news in the financial markets, making emotional rather than logical choices. This is empirically demonstrated by the 2008 financial crisis and the GameStop incident, where investors panicked in response to temporary losses, escalating market volatility.

The idea of overreaction in financial markets is further supported by Shiller's work on market irrationality. According to his theory, illogical market behaviour is frequently driven by emotions, narratives, and collective social psychology, proving that markets are not always rational. For instance, investors' decisions during the 2008 financial crisis and the dot-com bubble were influenced more by social and emotional reasons than by the fundamentals of the economy. Shiller's research sheds more light on how overreaction appears in financial markets by demonstrating that group psychology, emotions, and collective behaviour were major factors in these market oddities.

We may better understand how market overreaction appears in various financial events and how emotions, cognitive biases, and group behaviour impact market price movements by combining these data sets and theoretical insights. In addition to enhancing our comprehension of market irrationality, these examples and experimental data show how emotions propagate across the market, increasing volatility and leading to prices deviating greatly from their underlying values.

Finally, examine the Overreaction to Earnings Reports—a real-time pattern that plays out throughout Asian markets, where cultural values of status and reputation heighten responses to business performance. In nations such as Japan, where corporate honour is key, an earnings shortfall may result in severe sell-offs as investors worry about the company's image harm. In contrast, an earnings beat is praised, potentially driving stock prices to unsustainable highs. Beyond the data, however, the impression is what drives the response. Investors sometimes rely on a single earnings report as a clear indicator of a company's direction, even if it only covers one quarter. This response is a combination of financial judgement and cultural expectation, with corporations seen as pillars of societal identity rather than merely economic enterprises. In China, the scenario is similar but heightened by retail investors who enthusiastically react to both official and rumoured earnings news, often resulting in price moves that are well beyond what the fundamentals would imply. The overreaction here is a result of both numbers and national pride, particularly for major, well-known enterprises with symbolic market weight.

Asian markets are more than just financial entities; they also reflect the region's cultural, psychological, and social undercurrents. The trends we see— from the January Effect to the Flight to Quality—are more than just oddities or statistical quirks. They are tales of collective behaviour in an area where money interacts with tradition, emotion, and social identity in ways that go beyond statistics. Each of these patterns provides a glimpse into Asia's financial landscape, revealing a complex world in which markets not only follow economic rules but also dance to the rhythm of human behaviour, shaped by centuries-old customs, contemporary anxieties, and timeless desires for prosperity, security, and success. Finally, these impacts remind us that no matter how smart markets get, they are still driven by people—people who rejoice, worry, hope, and, most importantly, continue to shape the financial tides in new and exciting ways.

The emotional rollercoaster of overreaction and market anomalies reminds us that investing requires as much psychological awareness as it does numerical ability. Markets are not efficient value calculators; human emotions, tales, hopes, and fears influence them. The key to managing this rollercoaster is to recognise when emotions are driving choices, both yours and the market's. It is about avoiding the impulse to behave rashly, whether it is jumping into the hottest stock or bailing out of a sound investment because others are doing the same.

Investors must always contend with emotional factors that might cause overreaction and the formation of market anomalies in the dynamic world of financial markets. Even though these phenomena have been around for decades, a closer look at their applicability in the modern market environment is necessary, particularly in light of the emergence of increasingly complex market mechanisms. Once seen as trustworthy trends, the January Effect and the Weekend Effect have lost some of their relevance over time as a result of improvements in trading strategy sophistication and market efficiency. Even though these irregularities are still addressed in academic and investment circles, they might not have the same impact as they once did because algorithmic trading systems and institutional investors are constantly trying to take advantage of and eliminate any inefficiencies of this kind. These systems actively seek to correct price discrepancies brought on by emotional overreactions, and the advent of high-frequency trading and the growing number of experienced investors have made it harder for such anomalies to persist.

Arbitrage possibilities and algorithmic trading are two examples of market mechanisms that have been shown to be successful in lessening the influence of the emotional responses that frequently cause price volatility. For example, when mispricing takes place, arbitrageurs intervene by taking advantage of differences in asset values between marketplaces and bringing prices closer to their actual worth. Algorithmic trading can swiftly absorb market shocks and lessen the effects of irrational trading behaviour since it uses programmed algorithms to execute deals quickly. By acting as stabilising influences, these techniques and technologies limit the degree to which market dynamics can be impacted by emotional reactivity. Additionally, seasoned investors with a thorough understanding of investor psychology and market fundamentals are better able to see and respond to overreaction indicators, frequently taking advantage of these opportunities to profit from mispriced assets. As a result, although market abnormalities and overreaction may still happen, the sophisticated mechanisms that now control contemporary financial markets are gradually mitigating their effects.

A more complex environment has resulted from this change in market dynamics; while emotional outbursts still happen, they are swiftly subdued by institutional players' quick reactions and advanced trading techniques. Anomalies like the January Effect and the Weekend Effect may still pique market watchers' curiosity, but their applicability has surely diminished, underscoring the flexible character of financial markets and the continuous conflict between human psychology and technical advancement. The emotional rollercoaster of overreaction and market anomalies remains a constant reminder of the relationship between human behaviour and financial markets as investors grow more conscious of these shifts and modify their approaches.

Chapter 8

Overreaction: The Aftermath of Market News

Assume you are at a big music festival that spreads over a vast field, complete with tents, food stalls and stages. The weather is shining, and thousands of people are spread out around the grounds, having fun. Suddenly, you hear an exciting, frenetic murmur sweeping across the gathering. It starts tiny, with a few people turning their heads, then another group moves, and gradually, more people stampede in one way. You cannot see what is coming, but your heart begins racing. Perhaps it is a renowned singer doing a surprise performance, something fantastic you are missing out on, or just a rumour. You are presented with a choice: do you remain put, hoping that the enthusiasm will pass, or should you join in, just in case it is something incredible?

Emotion and Market News

Consider that festival to be the financial market, and those rapid, instinctual motions are driven not by festival attendees but by investors responding to market news. The most recent earnings report, an unexpected resignation by a CEO, a new piece of legislation—these are the whispers that sweep over the market like a ripple, morphing into waves that force investors to act in unison. Investors, like festival-goers who do not want to miss out on something unique, respond quickly, motivated by the fear of losing out on profits or being the only one left holding a deteriorating asset. It is an emotional rollercoaster—a gut response in which fear and greed outweigh logical understanding, resulting in a collective overreaction that drives prices well beyond where they should be.

This is the truth of overreaction, an emotional response that may cause stock values to skyrocket or plummet to unforeseen lows. In the excitement, it is difficult to see clearly; investors get caught up in the moment, carried along by the mob, much as a festivalgoer may rush to see the surprise act without wondering if it is really genuine. Later, as the dust settles and the truth is disclosed, investors reassess—sometimes finding that the action was warranted, other times realising that they overestimated or misjudged the significance of the news. The actual nature of market overreaction is revealed in these times of enthusiasm, as well as in the quiet that follows—often leaving behind a trail of overbought or oversold assets, ideal for those with the patience and discipline to wait out the commotion.

In the world of finance, news is what keeps investors on their toes—earnings reports, new government regulations, business scandals, and economic projections. These developments are like stones dropped into a peaceful pond, causing ripples that shift the market's surface. The markets, however, are defined by how investors respond to the news, not the news itself. Overreaction occurs when such ripples amplify into waves, fuelled by emotion rather than logical reasoning. It is a recurring dance—a rush of enthusiasm or anxiety in response to market news that drives prices well beyond what the fundamentals would suggest. When everyone hurries to purchase or sell, they are generally motivated by emotion rather than rationality.

The receipt of big news often sparks a response in financial markets, causing a ripple effect that spreads through investors like a wave of heightened emotions. When unexpected information arrives—whether it is a company's poor earnings report, a new regulatory regulation, or macroeconomic shifts—the first response is seldom calm or calculated. Instead, investors are subjected to a psychological pressure cooker. The first reaction to the news is visceral: sell out in terror or buy in with enthusiasm. Overreaction emerges in these high-tension situations. Human psychology is predisposed to see shocks as dangers or opportunities requiring immediate action. In the context of financial markets, this evolutionary drive manifests as an impulsive haste to act. Investors, attempting to either reduce losses or pursue profits, often respond without fully appreciating the news or its long-term ramifications, laying the groundwork for an overreaction.

The emotional character of overreacting may be shown most clearly following unfavourable market news. For example, if a well-known firm issues a bad financial report, many investors will instinctively sell before the situation worsens. This panic-driven response may set off a chain reaction, with one investor's sell-off spurring others to follow suit. The worry of watching an asset's value fall is infectious, spreading panic across the market. Rational investigation may reveal that the company's fundamentals are still intact, that this setback is just temporary, or that the business model is robust. However, the primal need to avoid perceived danger pushes prices much below their true worth, transforming what might have been a minor dip into a disastrous drop. This is the essence of overreaction: an emotional exaggeration of the real danger or reward, resulting in dramatic, sometimes unreasonable price fluctuations.

Social Media and Market Chaos

The involvement of the media is an essential factor that contributes to overreaction. Financial news channels rely on immediacy and drama; they are meant to capture the audience's attention. When news breaks, it is often accompanied by spectacular headlines that may elicit strong emotions. A title like "Tech Giant's Revenue Misses Expectations, Shares Plunge!" is designed not merely to educate but also to instil a feeling of urgency and panic. This results in an emotional feedback loop: investors read the spectacular headlines and respond emotionally by selling or purchasing. This generates additional news about the quick price swings, exacerbating the fear or exhilaration. The media, by emphasising both good and bad news, adds to a self-perpetuating cycle of overreaction, as investors are constantly assaulted with information that prompts rash judgements.

Social factors have an essential influence on the development of overreaction. Investors are not just reacting to news in isolation; they are also monitoring the behaviour of other investors, especially during times of market instability. When a significant price drop or spike happens, the presence of others taking extreme actions becomes a motivator. This social proof exacerbates overreaction—investors fear being left behind if they do not follow the majority. It is a fear-driven choice, not a sensible one. Seeing others sell makes an investor question their original evaluation, prompting them to join the sell-off, even if they do not entirely feel it is the proper decision based on the fundamentals. The emotional contagion spreads, and before long, a collective response occurs, propelling the market to extremes that are unrelated to any objective appraisal of the asset.

Overreaction may cause both short-term mispricing and long-term market distortions. When prices fall too much as a result of panic selling, it might take some time for confidence to recover, even if the original worries are unwarranted. Investors whose response has burned may become unwilling to reinvest, resulting in an undervaluation period that lasts long after the real danger has passed. In contrast, when overreaction pushes prices higher—perhaps owing to excitement over a new product or a high-profile announcement—the inflated values may result in bubbles. Investors who invest during the peak of this euphoria may find themselves holding inflated assets when the market ultimately corrects, resulting in huge losses. Overreaction is, therefore, cyclical in nature—it causes large price swings at first, followed by a delayed correction as investors rethink and readjust their judgements.

Consider a fictitious firm, GreenTech Innovations, which is about to introduce an innovative new sustainable energy product. Investors are ecstatic about early rumours of a new battery technology, sending the stock price skyrocketing. The news is initially optimistic: the technology has the potential to disrupt the industry, offering a greener and more efficient future. But then comes the earnings report, which falls short of expectations. Perhaps the corporation discloses that manufacturing costs are more than anticipated or that regulatory impediments are causing delays. Suddenly, the story shifts. Investors who were only minutes before excited to see the firm prosper are now hurrying to sell their shares, fearing losses. The same excitement that drove prices up in the first place is now driving them down in a quick, often illogical sell-off. In the rush to get out, rationality gives way to panic, and GreenTech's stock price plummets, much below what the company's true worth would imply.

This sequence—the original emotion, the exaggeration, and the reversal—represents the normal cycle of overreaction and correction. In the short term, markets behave like emotional adolescents, alternating between exhilaration and despair in reaction to the newest piece of gossip. And, although financial theory often assumes that markets are efficient and react rationally to new information, the reality is considerably messier. Market participants are individuals, and people are emotional. They overreact. They get into a panic. They allow fear and hope to cloud their judgement, resulting in substantial price movements that have no bearing on the underlying worth of the assets in issue.

It is crucial to remember that overreaction is sometimes illogical from an individual's standpoint. Assume you are an investor with a significant investment in a firm that unexpectedly discloses dismal profits. The prudent course of action could be to carefully assess the situation, weigh the long-term possibilities, and hang on if the fundamentals remain strong. However, if you see others selling and the price decreasing, the desire to participate becomes irresistible. This behaviour is influenced by what is known as "loss aversion"—the belief that losses harm us more than benefits. Seeing the value of your assets fall elicits an almost visceral response. The anguish of a prospective loss becomes too great to bear, and you sell without thoroughly assessing the benefits of the news in order to prevent more suffering.

The selloff starts, and it affects more than simply individual investors. Institutional investors, with their complex algorithms and legions of experts, are as prone to overreaction. Hedge funds, pension funds, and other significant players often have mandates that force them to reduce risk. When unfavourable news emerges, even if it seems overblown, these institutions may lower their investments to safeguard their portfolios from future losses. When a fund manager watches a position's value decline, the choice to cut losses and move on may seem sensible in the heat of the moment, especially if they have customers and stakeholders to answer to (Gans Combe et al., 2023). This institutional response may exacerbate the impact of overreaction, resulting in significant stock price losses that, in retrospect, seem unjustified.

A typical example of overreacting may be seen in the aftermath of the COVID-19 pandemic's first breakout. In February and March 2020, markets throughout the globe saw a rapid and catastrophic drop. Fear gripped investors throughout the world as nations started to enact lockdowns, and the extent of the virus became obvious. There was natural anxiety about the pandemic's effect on the global economy, with widespread uncertainty about how long it would endure and the extent of the damage. However, the pace and magnitude of the sell-off exceeded realistic estimates of economic impact. Instead, it created a self-reinforcing spiral: investors, terrified of additional drops, liquidated their shares, pushing prices lower, causing more anxiety and selling.

However, in the following months, the market started to rebound. Governments and central banks implemented large stimulus packages to provide liquidity and stabilise the economic outlook. By the end of 2020, several markets had recovered the majority, if not all, of their losses, with some even setting new record highs. The first overreaction—the frantic, emotional selling—had given way to a more measured view of the long-term economic consequences. Those who sold during the panic found it challenging to accept the quick rebound. It was a perfect example of the emotional rollercoaster that overreaction causes—a sudden plunge fuelled by panic, followed by a slow ascent as logic returns.

Figure 8.1. Market Performance During Initial COVID-19 Outbreak (Jan-June 2020)

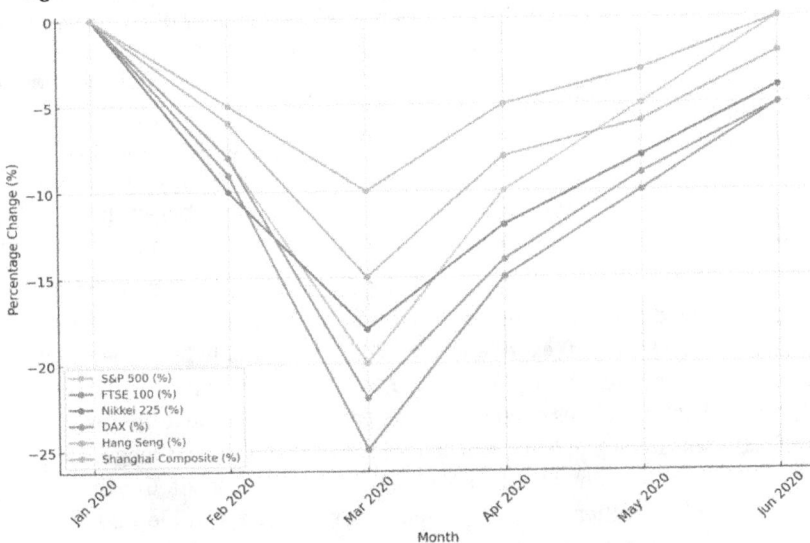

Source: Author's Work

In the annals of modern history, 2020 will forever be remembered as the year when an invisible enemy brought the world to its knees. The initial outbreak of COVID-19 was not just a health emergency; it was a seismic shockwave that reverberated through the global economy, rattling markets, shaking confidence, and leaving investors with an all-consuming sense of uncertainty. Imagine a tightly knit web holding the global economy together. In early 2020, that web began to tear, each rip spreading like lightning from one corner of the world to another. The world of finance, usually driven by numbers, data, and calculated risks, became a theatre of emotion, where fear became a more powerful driver than fundamentals.

Picture this: It is early February 2020, and investors are beginning to get nervous. The news of a mysterious virus that originated in Wuhan, China, is spreading across the globe. In boardrooms and trading floors, conversations quickly shift from growth projections and earnings to hospital capacity and infection rates. In this environment, investors did not have the luxury of rational calculations. Instead, they were bombarded with headlines of rising death tolls, collapsing supply chains, and entire cities locked down. The familiar hum of financial markets started to shift in tone—a growing dissonance hinting that the world was on the brink of something far worse than a mere correction.

By the end of February, that dissonance became an outright crash. The S&P 500, the barometer of American corporate health, began to nosedive. In a matter of weeks, it dropped by 8%, and then another 20% in March. What began as a concern about a virus in a far-off city turned into full-blown panic. In New York City, Wall Street traders watched as their screens filled with red, their minds racing with questions that had no easy answers: How far would this virus spread? Would governments be able to contain it? And perhaps most troubling of all—what would this mean for businesses, big and small? The S&P 500 was a mirror reflecting the fear and uncertainty spreading across America. Retail investors, pension funds, and institutions alike began liquidating positions, moving their money to safe havens as the market dipped lower and lower. This was not a time for careful analysis; it was a time for survival.

But the United States was not alone in this frenzied sell-off. Across the Atlantic, in London, the FTSE 100 experienced a similar story—only here, the numbers were even more dire. The FTSE dropped by 9% on February 20, 2020, but by March 12, 2020, the losses deepened to an alarming 25%. The drop was not just a reflection of global panic but also an indication of specific challenges faced by the UK. Already burdened by the uncertain aftermath of Brexit, the UK faced a crisis unlike any other. Businesses reliant on European trade and tourism were staring down a sudden collapse in demand, and the financial services industry, which formed the backbone of the UK economy, found itself on shaky ground. The world watched as London, a symbol of financial stability, grappled with a crisis for which it had no playbook.

In Japan, the sentiment was no different. The Nikkei 225, a representation of Japan's economy—a blend of high technology, automotive giants, and consumer goods—faltered. The Nikkei dropped by 10% in February, with losses worsening to 18% by March. Japan, which had always prided itself on resilience and adaptability, now found its key strengths turning into vulnerabilities. The intricate supply chains that were crucial to its industrial prowess were disintegrating overnight. Factories lay idle as global demand plummeted, and domestic consumption—a key economic driver—was crippled by fear of contagion. The March decline was more than just numbers on a screen; it was an emotional blow to a nation that had fought its way out of stagnation with determination, only to see its progress halted by an unseen enemy.

Further west, in Germany, the DAX—a symbol of European industrial might— saw a steep decline of 22% in March. The losses were emblematic of Germany's particular vulnerability during this crisis. Known for its manufacturing dominance, Germany found itself facing a unique predicament. The factories that formed the heart of the German economy producing everything from luxury cars to precision machinery, were shut down. Orders were cancelled, supply lines severed, and the famed efficiency of German industry was rendered powerless against the virus. Investors, once confident in the industrial prowess of Europe's strongest economy, now questioned whether the economic backbone of Europe could withstand such an unprecedented shock.

Across the Asian continent, Hong Kong, a bustling hub of finance and trade, saw the Hang Seng Index plummet. The Hang Seng fell by 6% in February and then nosedived another 15% in March. It was not just the virus that worried investors in Hong Kong; it was the political uncertainty that loomed over the city. Protest movements and tensions with mainland China had already strained the local economy, and now COVID-19 added a new layer of unpredictability. In the span of just a few weeks, a city that had thrived on certainty—where deals were made, and fortunes were built—was thrown into disarray. The image of Hong Kong as a financial powerhouse was suddenly clouded by the dual spectres of political instability and an uncontainable virus.

Even in China, where the virus originated, the Shanghai Composite Index saw significant declines—falling by 5% in February and another 10% in March. This was an extraordinary moment for China—a country accustomed to double-digit growth, where economic success was often a given. The entire machinery of the Chinese economy came to a screeching halt. The once-bustling factories, the ports, the expansive rail network—all of it paused. Investors fled, fearing a deep recession that could take years to overcome. But unlike in other nations, the Chinese government moved quickly and decisively, locking down cities, enforcing quarantines, and directing resources towards stabilizing the economy. By April, the Shanghai Composite began to stabilize. The Chinese government's response, though authoritarian, provided a level of stability that other countries were struggling to achieve. Investors began to trickle back, buoyed by the confidence that China, through sheer force of will, might lead the way out of this crisis.

The month of April marked a turning point. Across the globe, the panic began to subside, replaced by cautious optimism. Governments, realizing the scale of the economic catastrophe, injected unprecedented levels of stimulus into their economies. Central banks slashed interest rates, while governments rolled out fiscal measures aimed at supporting businesses and individuals. In the United States, the Federal Reserve stepped in, buying bonds and injecting liquidity to keep the financial system afloat. The S&P 500 started to recover, losses narrowing to -10% as investors found hope in the measures being taken. The market's rebound was not uniform, nor was it a signal that the crisis was over—but it was an indication that fear had begun to give way to reason.

In London, the FTSE 100 also showed signs of recovery. Losses decreased from -25% to -15% in April, as government furlough schemes and other interventions provided some degree of economic stability. The fear of complete economic collapse began to dissipate as people understood that, although the virus was not yet under control, the worst-case scenario might be avoided. Investors began to dip their toes back in, buying undervalued stocks and betting that the resilience of British industries would eventually shine through. Germany, too, saw a glimmer of hope in April. The DAX rose from its March lows, with losses reducing to -14%. The German government's commitment to support its workers and industries was a signal to investors that the worst might be behind them. Factories, although not yet at full capacity, were beginning to re-open, and the spirit of engineering excellence that defined German industry was showing signs of revival. Investors were cautiously optimistic, placing their trust in the ability of German companies to innovate and adapt, even in the face of adversity.

By June, the picture was beginning to look significantly better. The S&P 500 returned to its January levels, signalling a full recovery of the initial losses. For many, it was a sign of the resilience of the U.S. economy—a market that, despite all odds, managed to rebound and even thrive in a time of crisis. This recovery was not without its critics—some warned that the market was disconnected from the real economy, where millions were still out of work—but the movement in the indices was an undeniable signal of renewed investor confidence. China, too, saw the Shanghai Composite back at 0%, a sign that the Chinese government's aggressive actions had paid off. Investors were emboldened by China's ability to bring its factories back online and the speed with which the economy restarted. It was a demonstration of the power of central planning, where quick, decisive action could turn the tide in a way that democratic governments, constrained by debate and public scrutiny, could not easily replicate.

The market movements from January to June 2020 were more than just fluctuations in prices; they were the manifestation of human emotion—of fear, hope, uncertainty, and resilience. These fluctuations illustrated how interconnected the world truly is, with every headline and every action creating ripples that travelled across continents. As the pandemic progressed, the markets gradually adapted, investors adjusted to the new reality, and optimism began to take root once again. The rollercoaster ride of the markets during the first half of 2020 is a testament to the resilience of the global economy—a story of fear that gave way to hope, of collapse that gave way to recovery. And, ultimately, it is a reminder that behind every market movement are the stories of millions of individuals—traders, business owners, workers, and families—all of whom contribute to the global financial ecosystem, each responding to the challenges of an unprecedented time in their own way.

Overreaction does not necessarily imply a lousy occurrence followed by a sell-off, however. Positive news may have an equally dramatic impact, causing euphoria and pushing prices much beyond their inherent worth. When Tesla joined the S&P 500 index in late 2020, its stock price skyrocketed in the weeks before its entrance. Investors, pleased by the news and maybe caught up in the enthusiasm of Tesla's rapid climb, purchased shares in droves, driving the price much higher. The inclusion was a signal—a measure of legitimacy and achievement that contributed to Tesla's narrative of being the automobile industry's future. However, as the actual inclusion happened, the stock price levelled down, and many of those who bought during the excitement found themselves with shares at inflated prices. The response to the great news resulted in a price increase that could not be maintained after the initial euphoria subsided.

Another well-known example of overreaction is the "Flash Crash" of May 6, 2010. On that day, the Dow Jones Industrial Average dropped over 1,000 points in a matter of minutes before rebounding almost as rapidly. The steep drop was caused by computerised trading algorithms responding to market orders and selling pressure. As the algorithms spotted huge numbers of selling, they started to sell as well, causing a cascade effect that drove prices down at an alarming rate. Human traders, witnessing the quick decrease, stepped in, fearing a more significant market crash. The fast rebound that followed demonstrated that the initial response was exaggerated—there was no fundamental rationale for such a substantial reduction in prices. The Flash Crash demonstrated how rapidly overreaction may spin out of control, especially in a market dominated by algorithmic trading, which lacks the human capacity to halt and reconsider.

The role of the media in overreacting is also worth considering. In the age of 24-hour news coverage, any bit of information, no matter how little, may be magnified and distributed in only seconds. Headlines are designed to capture attention; terms like "market meltdown" or "stocks plummet" elicit strong emotional reactions. Investors who are overwhelmed with these stories are more likely to respond, either by buying into the enthusiasm or selling out of fear. The media does more than merely report on market occurrences; it also builds the narrative around them, often turning tiny swings into tremendous stories that may influence market behaviour. In a world where information travels at the speed of light, the risk of overreaction is higher than ever as investors respond to the newest headlines, often needing to understand the underlying context fully.

Overreaction is really about the confluence of information and emotion. It occurs when new knowledge, whether favourable or harmful, combines with the very human emotions of fear, greed, and uncertainty. In the wake of market news, investors must negotiate their feelings while attempting to extract the signal from the noise. Overreaction causes mispricings, which are equities that are either undervalued or overpriced as a result of an emotional response to the news. Mispricings might open up chances for individuals who can remain calm and sensible. Buying when others are afraid or selling when others are excessively optimistic requires a degree of emotional control that is tough to master but may be very rewarding.

Cases of Overreaction

The idea of overreaction is also linked to a more extensive knowledge of behavioural finance, which investigates how psychological variables impact financial decisions. Traditional finance models presume that investors are rational decision-makers who constantly use logic and reason. However, overreaction shows that this is far from true. Cognitive biases, or mental shortcuts, may affect investors and contribute to mistakes in judgement. Overreaction is often caused by the availability bias, in which recent events are given more weight than they merit, resulting in an excessive response. When bad news hits, it is natural to imagine that things will only get worse, just as good news might lead to even better times. These biases, which are firmly embedded in human psychology, account for the prevalence of overreaction in financial markets.

Overreaction may lead to value for the logical investor. When the emotional dust settles, prices often recover to levels that better represent the asset's fundamentals. This correcting process might take days, weeks, or even months, depending on the nature of the news and the strength of the first response. Overreaction might give an opportunity for those prepared to look beyond the immediate headlines to acquire inexpensive assets or sell overpriced ones. It is a technique that involves patience, discipline, and the capacity to stay cool in the face of market volatility. Warren Buffett's renowned admonition to "be fearful when others are greedy, and greedy when others are fearful" is directly relevant to the idea of overreaction. It is about recognising when the market has shifted too far in one way and positioning oneself to profit from the inevitable return to balance.

Overreaction is more than simply a financial problem; it reflects human nature. It tells the narrative of how fear and hope influence choices, how emotions may cloud judgement, and how the aggregate actions of millions of investors can cause market movements that defy rationality. Overreaction is followed by a time of adjustment, during which prices gradually match with reality and emotional highs and lows give way to a more balanced perspective of the world. It is a never-ending cycle, fuelled by the same human motivations that have continually moulded financial markets. Understanding overreaction is critical to understanding the markets themselves since it is at these periods of excess—whether exuberance or despair—that the actual essence of investment is exposed. It is more than just statistics and data; it is about people, with all of their faults and prejudices, attempting to navigate the intricate, ever-changing world of finance. And for those who can control their emotions and look beyond the noise, the aftermath of overreaction may be a golden opportunity.

In 2018, Malaysia saw a political change that shocked the country. During the May 9, 2018, general election, the opposition alliance, Pakatan Harapan (PH), removed the Barisan Nasional (BN) coalition from power for the first time in over six decades. This momentous changeover meant more than simply a change in administration; it foreshadowed the possible disruption of long-standing policies, sparking considerable conjecture and worry. Major political transitions are naturally uncomfortable for investors, who value stability and predictability. The market's quick reaction reflected collective anxiety—an overreaction fuelled by uncertainty about what changes might come with a new government.

Following the election, the Malaysian stock market underwent a severe sell-off. On May 14, the first trading day after the election, the FBM KLCI index declined by around 2.7%, losing nearly 40 points to settle at 1,850 points, down from 1,889 points before the election. This dip reflected investors' worries about the incoming government's approach to fiscal policy, big infrastructure projects, and foreign investment. The volatility index, a measure of market uncertainty, increased at this time, emphasising investors' emotional response to the political upheavals. Many investors, uncertain of the new government's intentions, liquidated their assets quickly, causing prices to fall sharply.

The building industry took the brunt of the overreaction. Pakatan Harapan promised to examine significant infrastructure projects launched by the previous administration, including the RM 55 billion East Coast Rail Link (ECRL) and the Singapore High-Speed Rail (HSR) project. This caused panic in the construction industry, with investors fearing outright cancellations or significant project delays. Stocks of firms actively engaged in these initiatives, including Gamuda, MMC Corporation, and George Kent, fell sharply. For example, Gamuda's share price fell from RM 4.08 on May 8 to RM 3.20 at the end of May, representing a more than 20% reduction. Investors moved in a hurry, not based on a rational assessment of project viability but on the speculative narrative that all large-scale projects would be delayed or cancelled, wiping away future income streams for these corporations.

Adding to the uncertainty, the banking sector saw decreases as predictions of less infrastructure expenditure led to concerns about weaker loan growth. CIMB Group Holdings Berhad, one of Malaysia's top banks, had its share price fall from RM 6.86 to RM 6.28 in the days after the election, representing an 8.5% decrease. Investors were worried that lower government expenditure would hamper economic activity, limiting credit growth and business borrowing. The emotional response to perceived policy alterations produced a market climate in which logical analysis took a backseat, and herd mentality resulted in widespread panic selling.

However, after the dust cleared, it became clear that the original worries were exaggerated. The new administration sought to reassure investors by defining its attitude to large-scale projects. Instead of outright cancellations, the emphasis was on renegotiating prices and increasing transparency. In August 2018, the government declared that it would continue with the ECRL project, although at a lower cost, which helped to restore investor confidence. Gamuda's share price, which had fallen during the initial uncertainties, started to rebound, returning to RM 3.80 by the end of 2018, as investors saw that the company's prospects were not as bleak as previously thought.

The broader market mirrored the transition from fear to recalibration. By the end of 2018, the FBM KLCI index had recovered significantly from its early post-election losses, hovering around 1,690 points. While the index remains below its pre-election high, its stabilisation suggests that investors are beginning to price in the new government's plans more sensibly, based on real budgetary choices rather than emotional conjecture. The construction industry recovered when it became evident that infrastructure building would continue, although with a greater focus on fiscal discipline.

Examining mechanisms like circuit breakers, risk management techniques, and the role of contrarian investors that aid in stabilising severe reactions to market news is crucial in addressing the market's overreaction. For instance, market circuit breakers serve as vital safety measures during times of increased volatility by automatically stopping trading to stop panic selling from getting out of control. By allowing for a cooling-off period, these mechanisms reduce the chance of future overreaction by giving investors time to reevaluate the issue more calmly. In addition to this, institutions employ risk management techniques like hedging and diversification to lessen the effects of sharp market fluctuations. These instruments serve as a buffer against the emotional fluctuations that could push markets to illogical extremes. Furthermore, contrarian investors function as a balancing factor in the market by buying when others are panicking or selling when others are exuberant. When the market returns to rationality, these investors frequently profit from mispriced assets and offer liquidity during periods of increased fear and overreaction. When combined, these tools and tactics are essential for preventing overreactions and preventing the market from deviating too much from its core principles.

A more thorough investigation of the precise triggers and the interaction between logical and irrational factors during crises is essential, even while the emotional rollercoaster brought on by market news is obvious, particularly during catastrophes like the COVID-19 epidemic or the 2008 financial meltdown. For example, during the 2008 financial crisis, the abrupt bankruptcy of large financial institutions sparked the initial panic, but not all market players immediately recognised the underlying problems—risky mortgage-backed securities and systemic breakdowns. A lack of transparency and an excessive reliance on models that understated the risk of such a crisis exacerbated the growing dread. While uncertainty and the threat of worldwide economic shutdowns drove the initial market collapse during the COVID-19 epidemic, logical responses from governments and central banks, such as stimulus packages and liquidity measures, sparked the later rebound. As investors transitioned from emotional reactions to more logical assessments of long-term economic effects, these measures assisted in stabilising markets. Both instances demonstrate the dynamic tension between fear-driven market movements and the stabilising effect of more measured, logical actions by combining an initial overreaction with a subsequent reasonable adjustment.

Overreaction in financial markets serves as a stark reminder that human behaviour, not economic models or quantitative studies, is what genuinely drives market movements. It is a complicated dance of emotions—fear, greed, hope, and anxiety—that causes people to purchase or sell in a frenzy, sometimes without stopping to examine the situation calmly. Whether it is the excitement of good news that propels an enthusiastic rally or the fear of bad news that triggers a massive sell-off, overreaction is a force that distorts reality, often resulting in price fluctuations that exceed their target. Markets, for all their complexity, are a reflection of human feeling, reflecting our tendency to act first and ponder later.

What makes overreaction so intriguing is its dual character. It causes moments of high danger while also providing a fantastic opportunity for those who can keep their emotions under control. The aftermath of overreaction is marked by a gradual and steady return to rationality, in which prices move away from the extreme highs or lows established by emotional transactions and drift back towards their underlying values. This rebalancing phase may be very profitable for savvy investors who see the opportunity in the mispricing caused by fear or enthusiasm. However, fighting the appeal of the herd or the pressure of panic needs discipline and an almost contrarian attitude, which is uncommon even among experienced investors.

The problem then becomes how to navigate the storm. Overreaction is unavoidable because it is embedded in the very fabric of human nature. We are not machines; we are emotional creatures, and when confronted with uncertainty or big news, our natural impulse is to protect or capitalise. But the market is a marathon, not a sprint, and patience, perseverance, and logic will finally prevail. Recognising overreaction and understanding that a price movement may be more indicative of group mood than underlying fundamentals is critical to being a successful investor. Investors may avoid emotional trading by taking a step back and evaluating market news objectively. Instead, they may use overreaction to create possibilities for development and profit, embracing the long game while others succumb to short-term noise.

Chapter 9

The Psychology Behind Biases: What Drives Irrationality?

Consider your brain to be a busy control tower, handling a constant stream of incoming signals such as ideas, sensations, memories, and information. It receives fresh data every second, and it uses shortcuts to make sense of this never-ending stream. Psychologists refer to these shortcuts as "biases." They are the unseen forces that guide our actions even when we believe we are acting rationally. Biases allow us to cut through the noise of the world, but they come at a cost. They warp reality, reflecting skewed images of what is truly going on, similar to the challenging funhouse mirrors at a funfair. We believe we view things objectively, yet biases limit our perceptions via our emotions, experiences, and subconscious habits.

Biases

Biases are subtle nudges that guide us to specific conclusions, frequently without our knowledge. Consider an investor checking the news and sensing the pulse of the market. They convince themselves they are making a rational decision, yet there are hidden biases at work. Confirmation bias whispers in their ear, prompting people only to perceive information that supports their existing beliefs. Overconfidence tells them that they have a distinct insight, a distinguishing feature that others lack. These prejudices are subtle; they do not make themselves known. Instead, they mix into our thinking, convincing us that every action we make is perfectly sensible.

We prefer to think of ourselves as rational creatures; after all, we take satisfaction in making judgements based on reason and facts. But the truth is that prejudices are built into the very structure of our thoughts. They are our brain's method of navigating an incredibly complicated environment. Imagine you are in the middle of a frenetic bazaar, with voices, colours, scents, and noises bombarding you from all directions. Without shortcuts and biases, your brain would be overloaded. Biases are the filters that help us concentrate on what is most important. They assist us in determining which signals are worth our attention, which courses to pursue, and which dangers to avoid. However, the same filters that save us from feeling overwhelmed may also lead us astray, distorting our judgement, particularly when making high-stakes choices like investing.

These biases are widespread, impacting everyone from the novice dipping their toes into investing to the seasoned professional managing millions. They are what make us human, what connects our behaviours and emotions, and they are complicated to overcome. Even when confronted with data that contradicts our ideas, our prejudices persist. They advise us to disregard the uncomfortable evidence and stick to our initial perspective. We do this because prejudices are comfortable. They provide us with a feeling of assurance and control, even when the reality is anything but. In the realm of investment, the illusion of confidence may lead to expensive blunders.

Biases are considerably more challenging to identify since they are profoundly emotional rather than just cerebral habits. They express our need to be correct, our fear of being incorrect, and our desire to fit in. They work silently, under the surface, influencing our perceptions of the world without our knowledge. They provide us with a vision of reality that feels comfortable and is consistent with our beliefs. This comfort, this subtle effect, is what gives prejudices their strength and risk. To properly comprehend our prejudices, we must lift the curtain on our thoughts, identify where our reasoning deviates, and accept the truth that we are not always the logical people we would like to believe. In the unpredictable realm of financial markets, biases are like invisible threads tugging us in various directions—sometimes aiding us, sometimes leading us wrong.

In psychology, biases are commonly referred to as "cognitive shortcuts" or "heuristics." These shortcuts developed to assist our ancestors in making rapid judgements in uncertain situations, such as choosing whether a rustling in the bushes was a predator or simply the wind. These mental shortcuts are still in use in today's financial markets, although they often fail. Imagine standing on the edge of a crowded marketplace, with hundreds of people yelling contradicting advice, attempting to make a choice that would affect your financial destiny. It is overpowering. When confronted with complexity, the human brain tends to gravitate towards the most straightforward, most efficient answer. And this is where prejudices flourish.

Irrational thinking is not a sign of weakness; rather, it demonstrates that our brains are a magnificent, complex, and beautifully human creation. To understand irrationality, we must first examine the brain, which is a complex network of systems that work together to keep us alive, prospering, and, yes, sometimes making bizarre, illogical judgements. Let us look at what occurs when we succumb to our biases—when the brain becomes its own worst enemy, leading us down perilous paths of overconfidence, fear, and herd mentality.

The amygdala, a tiny, almond-shaped cluster located deep inside your brain's temporal lobes, is a key part of this drama of irrationality. If your brain is a busy metropolis, the amygdala is the fire station, always on the lookout for any hint of trouble. In evolutionary terms, this made complete sense. When our ancestors roamed the savannah, the amygdala's role was to keep us safe by detecting possible threats—a lurking predator, the smell of something strange—and eliciting an instant, intuitive response: fight, flight, or freeze. Fast forward to today, and the same structure is still operational, scanning for threat and ready to respond. But the risks are no longer sabre-toothed animals; they are stock market volatility, breaking news about a financial catastrophe, or the concern that the value of our assets would plummet.

When the amygdala takes control, it effectively hijacks the brain. This is known as an "amygdala hijack," according to psychologist Daniel Goleman. Assume you are sitting in front of your computer, checking the market ticker on a particularly horrible day. Stocks are plummeting, and the numbers have turned red, indicating losses. Your amygdala perceives this as a danger; it cannot distinguish between a dropping stock price and a predator. It sets off alarms, unleashing a surge of stress chemicals such as adrenaline and cortisol. Your heart beats, your muscles strain, and the prefrontal cortex, the reasoning half of your brain, is virtually silent. This is the moment that panic selling occurs. When investors watch their portfolio's value diminish, they feel an overpowering impulse to "do something"—even if doing nothing is the wiser option. Although strong, the amygdala lacks finesse. Its purpose is survival, not profit. At that point, selling everything felt like survival.

The prefrontal cortex is the area of the brain where reason, logic, and sophisticated cognition exist. This region, positioned just below your brow, functions as the brain's control centre, carefully analysing possibilities, assessing risks, and making sound judgements. However, the prefrontal cortex functions slower than the amygdala, and its task becomes considerably more difficult under stress. When the body is inundated with cortisol, the prefrontal cortex fails to operate properly. It is like trying to concentrate on draughting a paper while a fire alarm goes off—it is tough, even impossible. The amygdala's sirens drown out the prefrontal cortex's calm voice, and in times of stress, even the most reasonable among us may make erroneous decisions.

The Form of Biases

However, irrational behaviour encompasses more than simply fear. Enter the striatum, a brain region involved in the reward system. If the amygdala is the fire station, the striatum is the casino, always seeking for ways to feel good, win, and get a reward. The striatum enjoys the adrenaline of a successful transaction. Every time an investor makes a solid decision, a surge of dopamine is released—dopamine is the brain's "feel-good" hormone, the same molecule that makes winning a game or eating a fantastic meal enjoyable. This incentive reinforces the behaviour, increasing the likelihood that the individual will repeat it. In financial markets, this may result in a deadly spiral of overconfidence, in which investors pursue ever-higher profits, persuaded of their own invincibility.

Overconfidence is one of the most common investment biases, and it derives mostly from the striatum's reaction to reward. When we achieve success, whether it is choosing a winning stock or correctly anticipating a market trend, our brains reward us with dopamine. It feels nice and generates a strong feedback loop. We begin to assume that our success is only due to our ability, that we have somehow tamed the turmoil of the market. We disregard luck, ignore chance, and make ourselves the centre of our own success narrative. This is known as the "illusion of control"—the notion that we have more control over outcomes than we do. The more successful we are, the greater this illusion gets, and the more inclined we are to take higher risks, frequently unaware of the danger. It is like going to a casino, winning a few hands of blackjack, and suddenly feeling like you are on a "hot streak." Rationally, you understand that each hand is separate and that the odds are always in favour of the house, but the dopamine surge convinces you differently.

The striatum is also responsible for another hazardous prejudice, confirmation bias. This is the propensity to seek out information that confirms our current ideas while rejecting facts that contradict them. Assume you have made a significant investment in a certain technology stock. You believe in the company's goals and leadership. Your brain, eager to reinforce the sense of satisfaction, will aggressively search out news stories, data figures, and expert comments that verify your conviction in the company's prospects. At the same time, it will ignore or minimise any unfavourable news—an analyst's warning, a dismal financial report, or a competitor's development. The striatum needs the dopamine rush that comes with believing you are correct, and it will do whatever to keep you feeling that way. This selective information processing might result in a false vision of reality, in which your ideas are constantly affirmed, even when the evidence says otherwise.

But probably the most old of all irrational behaviours is herd mentality—the need to follow the crowd. Evolutionarily, this made perfect sense: being part of a group increased your chances of survival enormously. The amygdala plays an important part in this sort of behaviour, perceiving others' activities as social signals that might indicate safety or danger. In financial markets, this is often known as FOMO—fear of missing out. Consider a situation in which a certain stock skyrockets. You read articles about it everywhere, social media is booming, and everyone around you is bragging about how much money they have earned. Your amygdala sees this as a possible threat—"Everyone else is making money, and if you do not act, you will fall behind." The pressure increases, and rational analysis takes a back seat. Instead of questioning whether the stock is a sound investment, you are motivated by a strong desire to be a member of the group, to avoid missing out on what seems to be a sure thing. This is how bubbles develop. Investors get engrossed in the excitement, driving prices to unsustainable peaks, only to confront a harsh reality when the bubble pops.

On the other hand, the amygdala is responsible for another tremendous force: loss aversion. Humans are naturally more sensitive to losses than to similar gains. The prospect of losing $1,000 is much more unpleasant than the joy of getting $1,000. This bias may lead to illogical actions, such as hanging on to lost stocks in the expectation that they will recover, merely because the agony of realising the loss is too severe. The amygdala produces a fear reaction when faced with the potential of loss, and instead of cutting our losses and moving on, we stay paralysed, waiting for a reversal that may never happen. The fear of loss impairs our judgement, making it harder to accept a loss and reallocate resources to a better opportunity.

At the heart of these biases is a conflict between emotion and reason, between the amygdala and striatum's quick, intuitive reactions and the prefrontal cortex's slow, deliberate computations. The prefrontal brain is where we balance advantages and disadvantages, as well as analyse the long-term ramifications of our choices. However, it is also the area of the brain that is most quickly overloaded. When stressed or under pressure, the prefrontal cortex may be sidelined, unable to compete with the sheer force of emotional reactions created by other sections of the brain. During times of market volatility, when prices are falling and uncertainty abounds, the amygdala often takes control, forcing us to make hasty decisions—sell everything, get out, protect yourself.

Understanding this internal fight is essential for understanding why we make illogical judgements. We are not naturally lousy investors, nor do we lack discipline. It is just that we are human. Our brains are hardwired to defend ourselves, seek rewards, follow the pack, and avoid loss. When predators or food shortages were our most serious challenges, we relied heavily on intuition. However, in the complicated, high-stakes world of financial markets, these instincts might mislead us. The task for investors is not to eradicate these biases—which is impossible—but to recognise them, understand where they originate from, and devise techniques to mitigate their influence.

Mindfulness techniques, which educate the mind to remain calm under duress, may assist the prefrontal cortex in maintaining control even while the amygdala fires warnings. Setting predetermined investment criteria, such as automated stop-loss orders, may help to remove emotion from decision-making. Diversifying portfolios and setting long-term objectives may help mitigate the effects of overconfidence and loss aversion. And, perhaps most crucially, realising that irrationality is a part of the human experience may help investors approach the market with humility, recognising that no one—not even the most seasoned expert—is immune to the biases that affect our ideas and behaviours.

Overconfidence is a notable example of how biases impact investor behaviour. Overconfidence is more than simply an exaggerated impression of one's powers; it is a fundamental misunderstanding of knowledge and control. Investors with overconfidence feel they have a degree of ability that distinguishes them from the rest of the market. They believe they have an advantage, a unique perspective that others lack. On the one hand, confidence is advantageous since it promotes risk-taking, which is necessary for more significant profits. On the other side, when confidence becomes overconfidence, it leads to neglecting risk, underestimating competition, and, eventually, making choices without fully appreciating the implications. Consider an investor who, following a series of profitable deals, feels they have a "knack" for forecasting the market. They double down, investing significantly in a single stock, confident that it will climb. When the market changes suddenly, their whole portfolio is in danger—not because the market is unpredictable, but because their faith in their talents caused them to take an unjustifiable risk.

Consider the example of Tom. Tom is a youthful investor in his late twenties from the United States who joined the market when everything was rising. His first foray into investing occurred during a flourishing bull market when it seemed impossible to choose a losing investment. Tom began modestly, purchasing stock in a technology business that had just revealed a promising new product line. Within months, his first investment had quadrupled. It seemed as if he had a golden touch; every firm he chose appeared to soar, and his portfolio increased dramatically.

Tom's acquaintances began to notice his obvious talent. They flocked to him for counsel, and he took pleasure in their admiration. His confidence grew uncontrolled, and he soon invested his whole funds in stocks, believing he had a recipe for success. He even began borrowing money to invest, confident that every action he took would bring him wealth. He would sit at his computer, watching the green numbers rise, feeling like a financial genius.

But once the market started to right itself, Tom's luck ran out. The equities that had previously surged started to sink, and Tom's leveraged holdings compounded his losses. He could not grasp it since he had been so confident. He clung on, sure that the market would swing in his favour and that his insights were too excellent to fail. He watched as his portfolio dwindled, his money vanished, and his obligations increased. Only then did he realise that his prior success was due to favourable market circumstances rather than his abilities. Tom's experience exemplifies how overconfidence may lead investors into dangerous areas. The first results are enticing—they convince investors that they have unique qualities, closing their eyes to the role of chance or broader market trends. It is not just about believing in oneself; it is about believing in oneself to the point where dangers are minimised, and prudence is ignored.

Confirmation bias, or the propensity to recall triumphs while forgetting mistakes, is a common cause of overconfidence. In Tom's example, he recalled every successful deal and ascribed it to his abilities while discounting losses as unfortunate or trivial. This selective remembering strengthened his notion that he was exceptional and that he had knowledge that others lacked. Over time, his unwavering confidence led him to take on excessive risk, overlook warning signs, and eventually suffer severe financial loss.

Confirmation bias is another important factor in investing. This bias happens when investors look for information that confirms their previous opinions while dismissing anything that opposes them. It acts as a filter, allowing just what you wish to view. Consider an investor who is firmly devoted to the notion that renewable energy equities represent the future. They study the news every day, but instead of taking a balanced approach that includes possible obstacles such as regulatory constraints or technical barriers, they only concentrate on good news. Every new solar project or government incentive strengthens their conviction and reinforces their choice to continue investing extensively in this market. This selective focus stops individuals from seeing the big picture, resulting in overexposure in a particular sector and a higher risk of severe losses if the market reverses.

Consider Susan, an investor in Germany, a firm believer in renewable energy. Susan has always been a supporter of green energy, so it was easy for her to invest in companies that shared her values. She started investing in renewable energy firms, thinking that these were the future. Susan followed every excellent piece of news, including additional government subsidies, technological improvements, and collaborations with large firms. Each good article strengthened her belief that she was on the right course.

However, as time passed, other obstacles emerged. Supply chain challenges, changing government rules, and increased competition from alternative energy sources all influenced the profitability of some of these enterprises. However, Susan opted to disregard the warning indications. She did not want to think that her assets were in jeopardy, so she blocked out any insufficient information. She ignored news pieces critical of the renewable energy industry and disregarded experts who said her stocks were overpriced. Instead, she concentrated only on the positive, increasing her assets anytime she saw a chance to do so. Susan's portfolio deteriorated because she could not see the bigger picture. Her confirmation bias caused her to create an echo chamber around herself, a universe in which her investments were sure to succeed regardless of evidence to the contrary. Susan was surprised when the market turned, and the values of her equities started to tumble. She had not planned for the potential of a downturn since she had never allowed herself to imagine it.

Confirmation bias stems from the human need to avoid cognitive dissonance— the mental pain caused by having opposing views. Susan's passionate conviction in the future of green energy clashed with the realisation that renewable energy may not be the surefire investment she had hoped for. To prevent this pain, she automatically filtered out facts that did not fit her viewpoint. This drove her to make more hazardous investments without fully grasping the sector's issues. Anchoring bias is another prevalent cognitive pitfall. This bias occurs when people make judgements based on the first piece of information they receive (the "anchor"). In investing, this often implies that investors get fixated on a specific price—whether it is the original offering price of a company or the amount they paid when they initially invested. Consider John, an investor who invests $50 per share in a potential technology business. Over time, the stock's price falls to $30. John, clinging to the initial $50 price, refuses to sell, confident that the stock would recover. Even if market circumstances shift and experts reduce their forecasts, John's anchor prevents him from lowering his losses. Anchoring bias makes it harder to adjust to new knowledge since the original reference point seems like the "true" value despite overwhelming evidence to the contrary.

Assume George is an investor in the United States who purchased shares of a big retail firm for $150 per share. George felt confident in the company's long-term viability, and things were going well for a time. The stock price even reached $200, and George felt justified in his choice. However, an economic slump occurred, and the retail sector suffered significantly. The company's stock price fell to $120, then $100, before settling at $80.

Despite shifting circumstances, George needed help to bring himself to sell. In his eyes, $150 was the "true" worth of the shares, and he was fixed on that price. He continued telling himself that the decline was just temporary and that the stock would soon return to its previous value. He refused to contemplate selling since doing so for $80 would entail accepting a significant loss, something George was unwilling to do. Even as the firm suffered from dwindling sales and greater competition, George clung to the $150 price point, unable to acknowledge the reality of the situation.

Anchoring bias often happens because the human brain needs a reference point while making judgements. When confronted with ambiguity, individuals tend to cling to the first piece of information they get, particularly if they lack the knowledge to assess the big picture. For George, the original purchase price of $150 served as his anchor, the amount against which all subsequent choices were judged. It clouded his judgement, keeping him from seeing the broader picture—that the company's fundamentals had changed and that holding onto the stock was no longer a good idea. This bias may be especially harmful in investing since it stops investors from reacting to fresh knowledge. The market is continuously changing, and what was previously considered a solid investment may no longer be feasible. However, suppose an investor is fixated on a specific price or conviction. In that case, they may be unable to make sound judgements about whether to cut their losses or move on to other potential prospects.

Biases in Trading

Biases flourish in the environment of herding behaviour, in which people copy the activities of a larger group, sometimes without fully comprehending the reason for those acts. Herding is profoundly ingrained in our brains, which is why, in uncertain circumstances, we seek others for guidance on how to act. In financial markets, herding may generate bubbles, in which asset values increase well beyond their fundamental worth because "everyone" is buying them. Fear of missing out drives investors to follow the pack, sometimes at the cost of reasonable research. Consider the cryptocurrency craze of 2017, when Bitcoin prices skyrocketed as more investors joined the bandwagon. Many people purchased Bitcoin not because they understood blockchain technology or believed in its long-term worth but because everyone else was profiting, and they wanted to be included. This kind of illogical herd mentality pushed prices to unsustainable heights, resulting in a significant correction when the bubble burst.

Assume Ethan, a novice investor, learns from a friend that a particular cryptocurrency is seeing tremendous growth. Ethan has always been interested in cryptocurrency, but he has never truly understood how it works. Still, he chooses to investigate. He connects to social media and finds several postings about individuals earning huge profits by investing in this new digital asset. Everyone seems to be talking about it—the excitement is apparent, and it looks like everyone is becoming wealthy overnight.

Ethan begins to feel the strain. He wants to be included, so he invests a considerable percentage of his resources despite his need for an understanding of the mechanics underlying cryptocurrencies. As more individuals like Ethan buy-in, the price rises, and Ethan begins to believe he made the correct choice. He even informs a few pals about his "success," and they agree to invest as well. The cycle continues: more individuals buy-in, pushing the price higher and higher. However, the market will soon alter. Negative news regarding regulatory crackdowns on cryptocurrencies sparks fear, and the price starts to decline.

Ethan, like hundreds of others, begins to watch his profits erode. He realises too late that he got swept up in the hoopla, motivated by the acts of others rather than a genuine knowledge of the investment. The price continues to drop, leaving Ethan with enormous losses.

Herding bias is motivated by the human desire for social proof—a psychological phenomenon in which individuals seek others for guidance on how to act, particularly in difficult circumstances. It is easier to defend an investment decision if everyone else is doing the same thing. Being part of the crowd provides comfort, even if the result is awful. Herding often causes market bubbles, in which prices rise due to collective excitement, as well as collapses, in which the fear leads to widespread selling. The irony is that, in both circumstances, crowd behaviour is often detached from the underlying fundamentals of the assets under consideration.

Their self-reinforcing character may also explain the persistence of these biases. When a bias results in a profitable outcome, it produces a feedback loop that encourages the investor to continue the same behaviour. Consider an investor who, against popular opinion, invests in a faltering firm because they believe they know something others do not—a sort of overconfidence. The firm recovers, and the stock price doubles. This achievement supports the investor's conviction that their hunch is better than analytical evidence, increasing the likelihood that they would overlook vital information in the future. The more times this occurs, the more deeply established the behaviour becomes, making it more challenging to identify and rectify the underlying prejudice.

Loss aversion is a strong bias that influences how investors perceive risk and return. It is not simply that individuals detest losing; studies have shown that the psychological agony of losing is nearly twice as intense as the joy of obtaining the same amount. This bias causes investors to make illogical choices in order to avoid losing money, even if doing so is in their best interests. Consider Emma, who paid $90 per share for stock in an automobile firm. The stock initially performed well, and Emma was happy with her purchase. However, the corporation encountered many issues, including supply chain interruptions, increasing competition, and dwindling revenues. The stock price continued to decline, going to $70, then $60, and finally to $45. Every day, Emma would check into her broking account and see the red numbers next to her investment, causing the knot in her gut to tighten.

Emma could not bring herself to sell. The prospect of locking in a loss was too painful—it seemed like accepting defeat. She convinced herself she would wait until the stock rebounded and that selling now would be a mistake. She held onto hope that the corporation would turn things around and the price would ultimately revert to her initial purchase level. However, the company's problems worsened over time, and the stock price fell more. Emma's loss aversion prevented her from making the reasonable choice to cut her losses and move on. Instead, she clung to a losing investment for much too long, expecting a comeback that never materialised. The anguish of losing money was so intense that it overshadowed her capacity to assess the issue rationally.

Loss aversion is profoundly ingrained in human psychology—it is a survival trait that developed to assist our forefathers in avoiding losing resources critical to their existence. In the context of investment, this fundamental fear emerges as an inability to accept losses, even when doing so is a reasonable option. Investors like Emma would prefer to stay on to a losing stock in the belief that it would recover than suffer the psychological anguish of realising their loss. This often leads to bad investment choices since cash is locked up in underperforming assets instead of being moved to more promising possibilities.

Availability prejudice is another prevalent bias that influences investor behaviour. It happens when individuals overestimate the probability of occurrences based on their ability to remember comparable instances. This bias may lead to irrational decision-making since recent or emotionally charged events have a disproportionate effect on how investors perceive risk and opportunity. Take Mark, an investor who experienced the 2008 financial crisis. The fear, the headlines, and the dramatic drops in the stock market are all vivid memories for him. Fast forward to 2020, when the COVID-19 epidemic starts to spread. The markets remain unpredictable, and Mark begins to see similarities between the present scenario and 2008. He recalls the dread and confusion of the financial crisis, and he starts to feel that the market is headed for another collapse. Mark liquidates his whole portfolio, confident that a considerable slump is on the way, and transfers everything to cash.

However, unlike in 2008, the markets recovered fast. Government stimulus packages and an increase in demand for technology equities drive a speedy recovery. The market reaches new highs, and Mark realises he has lost out on big profits. His choice to sell was motivated not by a realistic assessment of the circumstances but by the availability of memories from the 2008 catastrophe. The vividness of the encounter affected his judgement, causing him to overestimate the chance of a repeat incident.

Availability bias arises when the human brain makes judgements based on the information that is most easily accessible. In the complicated world of investment, where data are abundant, the brain takes shortcuts by focusing on recent or emotionally significant occurrences. This might cause investors to respond disproportionately to news or events that may reflect less considerable market trends. Mark's recollection of the 2008 catastrophe was so strong that he made a judgement based on fear rather than a fair appraisal of the market's possibilities.

These biases are not abstract concepts; they are pretty accurate and impact even the most experienced investors. The key to controlling prejudices is awareness. Understanding how these mental shortcuts function, why they originated, and how they appear in financial decision-making can help investors recognise when they are sliding into a psychological trap. It is not feasible to eliminate biases; thus, the goal is to reduce their influence. Rational investment involves ongoing monitoring, knowledge of one's mental flaws, and a willingness to question one's intuition, even if it is unpleasant.

It is impossible to completely predict or plan ahead while developing a personal investment philosophy. As previously mentioned, it is founded on experience and changes over time as one's perspective is shaped by exposure to the market and personal insights. As investors experience several market cycles and gain a better grasp of their risk tolerance, investing objectives, and personal preferences, the process is continuously improved. This philosophical evolution is dynamic rather than static, and it could alter as fresh insights and experiences are added to an investor's strategy. Driven by emotions and social pressures, herding behaviour frequently contradicts individual investment philosophies by causing irrational decisions that follow the herd rather than independent thinking. But as investors get more seasoned, they learn to stand up to the herd and stick to their own beliefs, realising that sustained success frequently necessitates a more methodical and less impulsive response to market fluctuations. An investor's attitude becomes a useful tool for negotiating the intricacies and avoiding the traps of rash decisions when the market landscape changes.

Recognising that people can remodel their neural pathways to mitigate these biases and promote more rational decision-making is crucial to effectively addressing the biases that drive our irrational responses. Developing mindfulness is one method to do this. In order to help people identify when their amygdala is taking over their thinking, mindfulness, a type of mental training, teaches them to be present and conscious of their emotional reactions. By engaging in mindfulness practices, people can retrain their prefrontal cortex to regulate impulsive, emotional responses, allowing them to make more deliberate, rational decisions. Investors are able to halt, think, and refrain from making snap judgements based on illogical desires or concerns because to their improved self-awareness.

Rethinking our thoughts can be greatly aided by knowledge and reasoning training in addition to mindfulness. People can improve their capacity to confront prejudices like confirmation bias and overconfidence by actively participating in logical thinking-promoting activities like puzzles, critical reading, or behavioural finance education. Investors who receive education are better equipped to recognise their cognitive traps, challenge their presumptions, and base their decisions on facts rather than feelings. Additionally, reasoning training helps people avoid the temptation of making snap decisions by teaching them to approach decisions methodically and thoroughly consider the facts and results.

In the end, it takes constant effort and a dedication to self-improvement to be able to rewire our brains and overcome unreasonable reactions. Over time, people can overcome the cognitive biases that cloud their judgement by implementing long-term tactics like mindfulness, education, and reasoning training. Even though we cannot completely avoid the impact of our neurological wiring, these techniques provide a potent means of bringing our feelings and reason into harmony, which can improve decision-making and possibly lead to better results in both the personal and financial spheres of life.

Chapter 10

Ripple Effects: Consequences of Irrational Investor Behaviour

The stock market is often depicted as a logical machine—a place where supply meets demand and facts, and value and prospects drive pricing. However, when the statistics are removed, what remains is significantly more human and unpredictable. Financial markets are a complicated web in which every thread links to another, and each move ripples out in waves, altering the landscape in ways that no one can completely predict. When irrational behaviour takes root, it affects more than simply individuals who make stupid bets. It reverberates throughout the system, causing ripple effects that may transform economies and even history.

It begins simply enough. A new opportunity arises—a fascinating breakthrough, a commodity that everyone suddenly desires, or an unstoppable market expansion. Hope spreads like wildfire, and others pile in. It is more than simply excitement; it is the belief that this is a once-in-a-lifetime opportunity that cannot be passed up. Conversations in coffee shops are rife with stories of easy money; those who had never shown interest in the market before are now glued to their screens, watching prices. It feels good—this common ideal, the idea that everyone is succeeding together. The enthusiasm is tangible, and it pulls more and more individuals in, causing the first waves of aberrant behaviour.

As more people join in, the first waves get more muscular. People start to feel invincible, as if economic rules no longer apply. What began as a trickle became a deluge. Financial institutions are not immune to the enthusiasm. Banks and lenders open their doors, providing cheap loans to everyone looking to get in on the activity. Mortgage firms, hedge funds, and investment banks are keen to join the game. It does not matter whether prices are skyrocketing or if individuals are purchasing assets they have little knowledge of; the promise of unlimited profits drowns out any warning signs. Credit becomes a magical wand, expanding buying power and adding gasoline to the flames. And just like that, the ripples become waves that propagate throughout the system.

As everyone rides high, the whole financial environment begins to alter. Regulators take a back seat, believing that the market knows best. Corporations join the excitement, growing wildly and incurring significant debt to fulfil their objectives. The vitality has an impact on everything—how policies are developed, how banks handle risk, and how people make decisions about their futures. The market continues to rise, and people persuade themselves that this is not a bubble but rather the beginning of a new age. It is no longer just about money; it is about belief, a seemingly unshakeable social narrative.

However, fissures develop with time. It may start with something modest, such as an earnings report that falls short of expectations, a rapid drop in an overvalued asset, or a change in interest rates that makes borrowing somewhat more expensive. The communal conviction that drove the boom starts to wane. It is quiet at first—just a few investors opting to cash out and seize their winnings while they still can. However, markets are unstable, relying as much on perception as on actual worth. Suddenly, the slight uneasiness spreads. Once confident, investors begin to feel anxious. The murmur of uncertainty becomes louder, eventually becoming a scream. People are rushing to sell and get out before it is too late.

The ripple becomes a rupture. Panic is infectious, particularly in the financial markets. When investors begin to withdraw in large numbers, prices fall, and dread rises. The waves struck the banks, lenders, and economic organisations that had fuelled the frenzy in the first place. Loans begin to fail, credit lines are withdrawn, and liquidity—the lifeblood of financial systems—dries up. What was once an overwhelming force of optimism has shifted into a downward spiral of dread and self-preservation. Investors, banks, and companies all scramble to cover their losses and minimise the damage. But the interconnection that once buoyed the market is now dragging it down. The ripples started with a few eager investors and have grown into a tidal wave that threatens the whole financial system.

The impact is quick and harsh. Companies that developed too rapidly are now unable to repay their loans. Projects are postponed, layoffs ensue, and bankruptcy is imminent. The larger economy is starting to feel the pressure. Small firms cannot get financing; consumers, hurting from losses, cut down on spending. A financial crisis is more than simply about markets; it is about people, employment, and the fabric of daily life. Suddenly, the ideal that everyone was seeking has turned into a nightmare, and the excitement that once fuelled talks has been replaced with tales of pain and sorrow. The human toll is staggering: families lose their homes, people lose their jobs, and the whole basis of economic stability begins to erode.

Following the first shock, there is a lengthier, more drawn-out aftermath. Governments intervene in a frantic attempt to avoid utter catastrophe. Bailouts are granted, emergency measures are implemented, and central banks flood the economy with cash. However, although these actions are required to stabilise the situation, they are not without consequences. National debt soars, austerity measures are implemented, and popular discontent develops. People's trust in financial institutions and government control has been shattered. The world today seems different—more cynical, wary, and damaged by the tragedies that have occurred. Once lost, trust is difficult to regain, and the consequences last for years, changing everything from regulatory frameworks to individual attitudes towards risk and investment.

Tulip Mania – 1637: A Nation Blooming into Madness

Imagine a period when flowers were more valuable than homes, and a single bulb offered riches beyond conception. In the 1630s, Holland was at the centre of the world's commercial networks, riding high on the money coming in from colonies all over the world. It was a nation of shipbuilders, merchants, and the type of optimism that inspired fantasies of unlimited prosperity. The tulip, a beautiful flower introduced from the Ottoman Empire with bright colours, entered our world as a sign of prestige and wealth. The Dutch were enthralled, and tulips quickly became more than simply a flower; they became a symbol of distinction.

The fever started as a whisper but developed into a roar that rang throughout the land. At its peak, in 1637, a single "Semper Augustus" bulb could fetch more than 10,000 guilders—enough to purchase a stately canal home in Amsterdam, or almost $1.2 million in today's figures when adjusted for buying power. According to historical records, tulip prices surged roughly twentyfold in six months. As individuals from all socioeconomic classes—farmers, artists, and merchants—joined the frenzy, bars became ad hoc marketplaces where contracts for tulip bulbs changed hands more often in a night than they did in soil.

The market rose due to leverage, which was fuelled by cheap credit and loans. People were borrowing extensively to buy bulbs, wagering everything on the belief that prices would keep rising. But, as quickly as it came, the craze dissipated. In February 1637, a single unsuccessful auction signalled the end. As fear crept in, tulip prices plummeted, and the market collapsed within weeks. A bulb may be worth a home one day and just a garden decoration the next. Between peak and crash, the tulip market lost more than 95% of its worth.

The aftermath was bleak. While it did not cause a collapse in the Dutch economy, hundreds of people went bankrupt, unable to repay the loans they had incurred to purchase bulbs that no longer sold. Trust in the market system weakened, and the Dutch government had to intervene to attempt to alleviate the turmoil by granting settlements to people saddled with bubble-related debts. The Tulip Mania left an indelible mark on Dutch culture, serving as a reminder of the hazards of uncontrolled speculation.

South Sea Bubble – 1720: Britain's Delusion of Endless Riches

The year was 1720, and the streets of London were alive with rumours of great riches. Britain, bolstered by its rising colonial strength and naval dominance, was drawn to the South Sea Company. Given a monopoly on commerce with South America, the firm promised enormous riches in the New World. The government supported it, and this sanction gave the project an air of invincibility. What started as cautious optimism quickly turned into full-fledged exhilaration, fuelled by promises of gold and wealth beyond imagination.

The South Sea Company's shares were initially valued at £100, but by the spring of 1720, they had risen to £500, and by June, they had almost reached £1,000—a tenfold gain in only a few months. During this time, even Isaac Newton, the brilliant mathematician, became swept up in the hoopla. Newton allegedly bought early and profited before re-entering the market at its height, only to lose over £20,000 when the bubble burst, which is equal to more than £4 million today. The rapid price increase pulled in not just the affluent but also the middle class and the poor, who sold property and borrowed money to invest in a corporation that was purportedly too large to fail.

In truth, the South Sea Company needed a conceivable method of earning the anticipated earnings. Much of the trade never occurred, and the company's worth was a house of cards. By September 1720, rumours circulated that the firm was unable to fulfil its lofty claims. Panic ensued. Within weeks, the share price fell from about £1,000 to around £150, wiping away fortunes and leaving numerous investors penniless. The collapse of the bubble wiped off around £500 million in market value, which is equivalent to £100 billion today, throwing the nation into financial catastrophe.

The following was marked by massive controversy. Investigations indicated that the company's directors cooperated with government officials, utilising insider knowledge to sell their stock before the collapse. The British economy failed to recover, and public faith in financial markets was severely eroded. Parliament enacted the "Bubble Act" to prohibit such speculative schemes, and many famous persons engaged in the bubble were shamed. The South Sea Bubble was a clear lesson in the hazards of rampant speculation, as well as a terrifying reminder of how even the mightiest may fail when greed closes their eyes to reality.

Chinese Stock Market Crash – 2015: The Rise and Fall of the Everyday Investor

In 2015, China evolved into an economic superpower, lifting hundreds of millions out of poverty and creating a booming middle class ready to invest in their future. The Chinese government, eager to build its financial markets, urged residents to participate in the stock market. From July 2014 to June 2015, the Shanghai Composite Index skyrocketed, tripling in value and peaking at more than 5,100 points. It was a spectacular ascent that seemed unstoppable, and millions wanted a piece of it.

By the middle of 2015, more than 90 million new broking accounts had been opened—more than Germany's total population. Many of these investors were first-timers enticed by the promise of fast and easy money. According to statistics from China's Securities Regulatory Commission, over 80% of transactions in early 2015 were made by individual investors, many of whom leveraged their wagers with borrowed funds. It was typical for investors to borrow up to three times their money to buy stocks, believing that the government would never allow the market to tumble.

However, markets are fickle. The first hints of instability surfaced in June 2015, when the Shanghai Composite Index started to sway. By July, the first little decline had developed into a plummet, with the stock losing more than 30% of its value in a matter of weeks. Within a month, the market had lost more than $3 trillion in value, which is almost comparable to Germany's whole GDP. The government reacted with severe measures, including banning trading for over half of the equities listed, infusing liquidity into the market, and encouraging significant shareholders not to sell.

Despite these steps, the harm had already been done. Millions of investors lost their life savings, and the dream of stock market success became a national nightmare. The disaster revealed the vulnerability of China's financial systems and underlined the dangers of a system in which market speculation was highly driven by government policy and social media hype. The repercussions changed China's financial regulatory environment, prompting authorities to prioritise stability and decrease the hazards of speculative trading. It was a terrible lesson for the world's second-largest economy, a warning that no market, no matter how powerful, can defy gravity indefinitely.

COVID-19 Pandemic – 2020: The Rollercoaster Ride of Pandemic Markets

It was unlike anything the world had ever seen. Fear rocked the financial markets in early 2020 as COVID-19 spread worldwide. The S&P 500 fell 34% from its February peak to its March low, one of the fastest falls in history. Within weeks, $18 trillion in global equities' worth had disappeared. Companies closed, millions of people lost their jobs, and whole sectors risked collapse. The crisis highlighted how interconnected—and vulnerable—the global economy was.

Despite the carnage, there was an astounding recovery. To prevent an economic meltdown, governments and central banks implemented a slew of stimulus measures. The Federal Reserve in the United States lowered interest rates to near-zero levels and poured billions of dollars into the banking sector. Governments throughout the globe implemented stimulus programs worth more than $16 trillion. The outcome was an unusual rush of liquidity, sending markets back up. By the end of 2020, the S&P 500 had not only recovered, but had set new record highs, completing the year up more than 16%.

Certain areas, including technology and healthcare, emerged as apparent winners. Companies like Amazon, whose stock price increased by 76% in 2020, and Zoom, which increased by 400%, emerged as heroes of the new pandemic-driven economy. According to Statista, Zoom's daily meeting attendees rose from 10 million in December 2019 to more than 300 million in April 2020. Investors rewarded these firms generously, sending market values into the hundreds of billions.

However, the epidemic also caused a significant increase in retail commerce. Platforms like Robinhood saw a rise in new accounts, while social media platforms like Reddit is WallStreetBets emerged as a new kind of market force. In January 2021, the now-famous GameStop short squeeze—driven by retail investors and fuelled by internet forums—boosted the stock price by 1,600% in a couple of weeks. This speculative frenzy demonstrated how mood, rather than fundamentals, might cause substantial market moves.

By the end of 2020, it was evident that the pandemic had not only affected the global economy but also changed the nature of investment. Markets, bolstered by stimulus and propelled by optimism, seemed removed from the harsh economic realities that millions suffer. It was a rally that emphasised the fragility of financial markets as well as the strength of collective conviction and emotional response. For many, the pandemic-driven market rollercoaster served as a sharp reminder that the gap between exhilaration and misery may be bridged in the blink of an eye.

Irrational behaviour has far-reaching consequences that do not just go away. They cause long-term shifts in how individuals see markets, money, and opportunity. The lessons learnt in the aftermath of a catastrophe are profound, yet history has repeatedly shown that these lessons are often forgotten. A new generation develops, one that has forgotten the suffering of the last catastrophe, and the cycle starts again. It is a never-ending dance of hope and terror, hopes and illusions. Financial markets are not cold, calculating machines; they are life, breathing creatures influenced by human emotion. Every choice, every transaction, every moment of exhilaration or terror causes waves throughout the system, affecting countless lives. Knowing these ripples—how they emerge, expand, and crash—means more than simply knowing money. It is about understanding ourselves—our aspirations, anxieties, weaknesses, and limitless ability to imagine.

GameStop and the Meme Stock Mania of 2021

Figure 10.1 illustrates the dramatic rise and fall of GameStop's stock price during the infamous "Meme Stock Mania" of early 2021. It shows how the price surged from $17.25 in early January to a peak of $483 by January 28, only to fall back to $51.20 by mid-February. This rapid fluctuation was a direct consequence of irrational investor behaviour, driven by a combination of retail investor enthusiasm, social media-fuelled hype, and institutional short positions.

The story of GameStop's meteoric rise in early 2021 was not just a tale of stock prices and market movements—it was a cultural and economic phenomenon that gripped the world's attention. The financial spectacle had the intensity of a high-stakes drama, complete with protagonists, antagonists, and plot twists that even the most imaginative novelist could not have crafted. It was a saga that pitted the so-called underdogs—ordinary retail investors—against powerful Wall Street hedge funds. It drew a line between two worlds that rarely meet: the established titans of finance, entrenched in their strategies and models, and an impassioned group of amateur traders with a smartphone in hand, a rebellious spirit, and a thirst for change.

Figure 10.1. GameStop Stock Price Surge During Meme Stock Mania (Jan-February 2021)

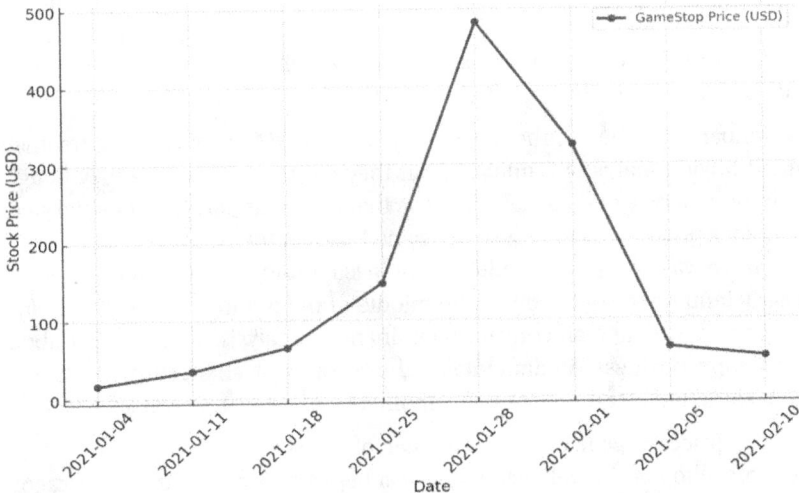

Source: Author's Work

It all began in the unlikeliest of places: Reddit, a sprawling online forum known for its diverse communities. Nestled within Reddit was r/WallStreetBets, a community of more than two million traders and amateur investors who embraced a high-risk, high-reward approach to investing. For them, Wall Street was not an institution to be revered—it was a target, a bastion of power that they had long been excluded from. They called themselves "degenerates," embracing the high-risk, almost reckless nature of their investments with a sense of humour that was as dark as it was captivating. And this time, their target was GameStop, a company whose nostalgia pulled at their heartstrings.

GameStop was a relic of the past, a company that sold video games in physical stores—an increasingly outdated concept in a world moving towards digital downloads and streaming services. It had become the quintessential underdog, with many hedge funds and institutional investors betting against it. In fact, these hedge funds had shorted more than 100% of GameStop's outstanding shares, a staggering number that reflected their absolute confidence in the company's inevitable decline. The sentiment was clear: GameStop was not going to survive the digital revolution. It was just another outdated business model on the path to extinction.

But the members of WallStreetBets saw something different. They saw an opportunity—not just to make money, but to send a message. In the eyes of this community, the hedge funds represented everything wrong with the financial system. They saw the shorts as greedy bets made by powerful institutions that profited at the expense of struggling companies and everyday investors. GameStop became a symbol, a rallying point for a movement that transcended financial motives. It was a chance to turn the tables, take on the titans of finance and show that the little guys could have power too. It was a perfect storm—a combination of financial opportunity, populist sentiment, and the desire to belong to something meaningful and significant.

As January 2021 began, the rallying cry went out. Members of WallStreetBets started buying shares of GameStop, but they did not stop there—they bought call options, a type of financial derivative that would amplify the potential gains if the stock price rose. The movement gained momentum, and soon, GameStop's stock price was rising—not gradually, but in leaps and bounds. From under $20 in early January to over $100 by the middle of the month, the stock was on a trajectory that defied all conventional financial analysis. This was not about GameStop's business fundamentals—those had not changed at all. It was about something far more powerful: momentum, belief, and collective action.

As the price surged, FOMO—the Fear of Missing Out—began to kick in. Investors who had initially been sceptical began to jump on the bandwagon. Why not? The price was rising, and every day brought new stories of people making huge profits. The movement spread from Reddit to Twitter, TikTok, and beyond. Suddenly, everyone wanted a piece of GameStop. It was not just about money—it was about being part of a moment, part of something that felt historic. People who had never bought a stock in their lives were opening brokerage accounts, buying shares of GameStop, and joining in the excitement. It was the democratization of finance in its most explosive form—a movement powered by the masses, enabled by technology, and inspired by the idea that, just maybe, they could beat Wall Street at its own game.

The hedge funds, meanwhile, found themselves in an increasingly precarious position. They had shorted GameStop stock, betting on its price falling. But as the price rose, they were faced with mounting losses. The higher the price went, the more they had to pay to buy back the shares they had borrowed to cover their short positions. It was a classic short squeeze, one that was becoming more painful by the day. The squeeze was amplified by the use of call options, which forced market makers to buy GameStop stock to hedge their positions, creating a feedback loop that drove the price even higher. What had started as a small movement on Reddit had turned into a financial juggernaut, one that was forcing some of the most powerful hedge funds in the world to their knees.

Melvin Capital, one of the hedge funds with a large short position in GameStop, was hit particularly hard. The fund faced massive losses as GameStop's stock price climbed, ultimately needing a $2.75 billion cash infusion from other hedge funds to stabilize. To the members of WallStreetBets, this was a victory—a sign that their movement was working. It was not just about money anymore; it was about proving a point. They had taken on the giants of Wall Street, and for once, the giants were losing.

By January 28th, GameStop's stock had reached an astonishing $483 per share. The frenzy was at its peak. News outlets around the world were covering the story, and it seemed like everyone was talking about GameStop. The excitement was palpable, but so too was the sense of impending doom. The price had been driven so high, so quickly, that it was clear it could not last. But the members of WallStreetBets were not backing down. They urged each other to "hold the line," to keep buying and refuse to sell, even as the risks grew. It was a test of wills—a standoff between ordinary investors and the institutions that had long held sway over the markets.

Then came the turning point. On January 28th, several brokerage platforms, most notably Robinhood, imposed restrictions on trading GameStop and other "meme stocks." Retail investors could no longer buy shares—they could only sell them. To the members of WallStreetBets and many other retail investors, this felt like a betrayal. Robinhood, a platform that had marketed itself as democratizing finance for all, seemed to be siding with the very institutions that they were trying to fight. The outrage was immediate. Social media exploded with accusations of market manipulation, and there were calls for investigations. The idea that Robinhood was protecting hedge funds at the expense of retail investors struck a chord, feeding into the narrative that the financial system was rigged in favour of the wealthy and powerful.

The restrictions had an immediate impact. With the buying pressure gone, GameStop's stock price began to fall. By early February, it was back down to $50 per share. The fall was as swift as the rise had been, and the financial and emotional toll on many retail investors was significant. For those who had bought in at the peak, the losses were devastating. The euphoria of seeing their investments soar was replaced by the crushing reality of watching those gains evaporate. It was a painful reminder of the risks of speculation, of the dangers of following the herd, and of the unforgiving nature of the financial markets.

But even as the price fell, the impact of the GameStop saga continued to resonate. It led to congressional hearings, where Robinhood's CEO, hedge fund managers, and others were called to testify about what had happened. It raised questions about the fairness of the financial system, the role of social media in driving investor behaviour, and the responsibilities of brokerage platforms. For many, it was a wake-up call—a stark illustration of how emotion, rather than rational analysis, can drive financial decisions, and how quickly things can spiral out of control when those emotions take over.

For the members of WallStreetBets and the broader retail investing community, the GameStop saga was about more than just money. It was about power, about taking a stand against a system that they felt was rigged against them. It was about proving that, for once, the small investors could make a difference, that they could take on the giants of Wall Street and win—at least for a moment. It was about belonging, about being part of something that felt significant and historic. And for many, it was worth the risk, even if the financial outcome was not what they had hoped.

The ripple effects of the GameStop mania went far beyond the individuals who bought and sold the stock. It led to a broader discussion about the democratization of finance, about the role of social media in shaping market movements, and about the power dynamics between institutional and retail investors. It exposed deep vulnerabilities in the financial system, vulnerabilities that could be exploited when collective action and emotion intersected in the way that they did with GameStop. It showed that in the age of social media and commission-free trading, the traditional rules of investing could be upended in the blink of an eye.

The GameStop story is a powerful reminder of the complexities of financial markets. On the surface, markets may seem like rational mechanisms driven by data and analysis, but beneath that surface lies a world of emotion, narrative, and psychology. The rise and fall of GameStop was not about earnings reports or future cash flows—it was about fear, hope, rebellion, and the thrill of being part of something bigger. It was about the power of community, the influence of social media, and the emotional forces that drive us all. And in the end, it was a story that captivated the world, not because of the numbers on a screen, but because of what those numbers represented—a challenge to the status quo, a fight for fairness, and the belief that, for once, the little guys could make a difference. It is a story that will be remembered as a turning point, a moment when the power dynamics of the financial markets were called into question, and a new chapter in the history of investing was written.

Even in the face of emotions and market volatility, investors must take the initiative to create techniques that improve their decision-making process in order to effectively control irrational behaviour. Developing self-awareness and mindfulness is one of the most important strategies for overcoming this obstacle. Investors might learn more about the psychological factors affecting their choices by routinely considering their emotional reactions and prejudices. This enables people to identify when their behaviour is motivated by herd mentality, fear, or greed rather than reasoned analysis. Before making snap decisions, investors can benefit from pausing to evaluate their views by incorporating techniques like journaling or meditation. Furthermore, it is essential to have a well-defined, long-term investing strategy. This approach should help investors resist the urge to follow the herd during speculative bubbles by concentrating on objectives rather than ephemeral market swings. Establishing clear guidelines for purchases, sales, and portfolio modifications can lessen emotional responses and offer a logical foundation for choices.

Diversification is another successful strategy. Investors might lessen the chance of suffering significant losses as a result of illogical market fluctuations by distributing their investments over several asset classes, sectors, and geographical areas. In addition to lowering risk, diversification supports a more measured, long-term strategy for accumulating wealth. Additionally, investors should refrain from using leverage excessively because borrowing money to make investments can magnify gains and losses, making downturns more stressful emotionally and causing irrational behaviour. Dollar-cost averaging, a method in which investments are made in predetermined amounts at regular intervals, independent of market conditions, can also be advantageous in volatile markets. This strategy avoids emotional reactivity to price fluctuations and mitigates the effects of market volatility.

Investors should also familiarise themselves with psychological pitfalls and cognitive biases. Investors can spot illogical actions by being aware of typical biases, including overconfidence, loss aversion, and the anchoring effect. Fostering a more knowledgeable, logical attitude to investing can be greatly aided by working with financial advisors that offer unbiased viewpoints, attending workshops, or interacting with financial education materials. Last but not least, investors can remain robust in the face of market volatility by keeping a healthy financial cushion and avoiding lifestyle inflation. This will enable them to stick to their plans without having to liquidate assets in times of panic. Investors can lessen the detrimental effects of illogical behaviour on their financial well-being by putting these techniques into practice and developing a more careful and rational approach to portfolio management.

Chapter 11

Breaking Free From Herding, Overconfidence, and Overreaction

Investing may seem like sailing a large sea, where the waves of market movements and crowd behaviour are so powerful that they can carry us away without our knowledge. Herding, overconfidence, and overreaction are the currents that drag us down, distort our judgement, and cause us to follow rather than lead. What if there was a method to overcome these influences and make clear, purposeful decisions? This chapter is about reclaiming our power, breaking free from the behaviours that keep us back, and charting a new course with daring but realistic tactics.

Building a Personal Investment Philosophy

Imagine sailing over a large ocean without a compass. You may begin with confidence, but as the tides of shifting trends and investor attitudes mount, your path becomes uncertain. A personal investing philosophy serves as a compass, an anchor that steers you through choppy financial seas. At its foundation, your philosophy determines who you are as an investor, what you value, and the ideas that guide your choices. Are you a long-term investor, or do you want growth with modest risk? Do you believe in sustainable investment, or do you want to maximise profits regardless of sector? Your philosophy addresses these issues by giving a set of principles that keep you grounded during times of turmoil.

Developing your investing philosophy is not about enforcing complex rules but about building a framework that allows for decision-making in every market circumstance. Begin by assessing your objectives, risk tolerance, and hobbies. Consider issues such as: "Am I investing to build wealth over decades, or am I focused on income for immediate needs?" Additionally, "Do I want to invest in sectors that align with my values?" Answering these questions helps you build a mental blueprint. For example, if your philosophy emphasises durability and consistent development, you will be less likely to follow high-risk trends. Every financial choice should be evaluated through this perspective. Over time, this mindset becomes second nature, steering you away from short-term desires and connecting your activities with a vision that is uniquely yours.

The benefit of a personal investing philosophy is that it is flexible. As your life circumstances change, your philosophy may evolve to meet your needs and ideals. However, it should always be constant enough to keep you grounded and remind you that the market is a long-term trip rather than a sprint. In moments of market euphoria or fear, your philosophy serves as a guidepost, keeping you on track when others deviate. This strategy fosters a feeling of independence, allowing you to act from conviction rather than responding to market noise.

Transforming Emotion into Insight

We frequently think of investing as a logical activity, yet it is very emotional. Every choice we make is influenced by our emotions, from the excitement of an enormous success to the dread of a quick loss. These emotions, if left uncontrolled, might lead to rash decisions that contradict our long-term plan. Mindfulness is very useful in this context. Mindfulness enables us to notice our thoughts and emotions without judgement, allowing us to see when we are responding out of fear, greed, or impatience rather than through rigorous thinking.

Mindfulness is like incorporating a "pause button" into your decision-making process. When your portfolio falls, mindfulness helps you to take a step back, breathe, and evaluate your emotions before acting. Are you inclined to sell out of fear, or is your choice consistent with your investing objectives? Learning to discern between these emotions and truth is critical for avoiding rash actions that might ruin your portfolio.

One technique to cultivate mindfulness is to set aside time each day to check your portfolio in a peaceful, distraction-free location. During this time, pay attention to how market changes affect your emotions. Do you feel calm, nervous, or overconfident? By recognising these emotions, you may obtain insight into how they influence your behaviour. Another helpful approach is to journal your investing choices, capturing not just the "what" but also the "why" behind each decision. This habit keeps track of your mentality, allowing you to see trends in your decision-making that can be adjusted over time.

Mindfulness is about developing emotional resilience. Markets are naturally volatile, and this technique enables you to adapt rather than react. It fosters a calm, measured mentality, transforming fear into observation and impulsiveness into deliberate action. Mindfulness does not eradicate emotions but instead converts them into awareness, providing you with an excellent tool for making balanced choices that line with your long-term goals.

A Defense Against the Echo Chamber

The emergence of personalised algorithms means that we are often bombarded with information that confirms our pre-existing ideas. If you are in a social circle or online group that is very positive about a particular industry, it is simple to embrace that optimism without considering opposing viewpoints. However, investing without varied viewpoints is like driving with blinkers on—you overlook the dangers and possibilities that are outside your range of vision. Breaking out from herding entails actively seeking out diverse perspectives, disputing preconceptions, and accepting opposing thoughts.

Diverse viewpoints are critical because they expose you to dangers and opportunities that you may otherwise miss. If you are heavily invested in tech companies, interacting with investors who specialise in other sectors, such as commodities or healthcare, might help you better understand possible market risks and movements. Reading research from several sources, following thought leaders with opposing viewpoints, and conversing with investors from all backgrounds all help to create a more balanced perspective.

Taking and defending an opposing perspective is an intense exercise. This compels you to question your preconceptions and explore the validity of alternative ideas. For example, if you believe in renewable energy's long-term expansion, research sceptics' arguments. You do not have to agree with them, but knowing their point of view will allow you to make better-balanced judgements. By broadening your expertise, you become less dependent on popular opinion and more confident in your analysis, allowing you to make judgements based on a more complete, more precise picture of the market.

Rules for Rational Decisions

The volatility of financial markets often leads us to act on impulse. Whether it is panic selling during a downturn or FOMO (fear of missing out) purchasing during a rise, these emotions may result in expensive blunders. Predefined investing triggers and guardrails provide a disciplined approach to navigating these emotions, allowing you to make choices based on reasoning rather than gut impulses. Triggers and guardrails are rules that you establish in advance to determine whether to purchase, sell, or hold an investment depending on specified criteria.

Assume you have invested in a company with a projected price rise of 20%. Instead of monitoring the price every day and discussing whether to sell, you may establish a trigger that will automatically sell the stock when it reaches your target price. Similarly, if you own an asset that declines by a specific percentage, a specified trigger might assist you in deciding whether to sell or retain based on your risk tolerance. These guidelines are particularly beneficial for avoiding overreaction since they create a structure that enables you to stay to your strategy even when market circumstances are chaotic.

Setting guardrails does not remove risk, but it does give limits that ensure your actions are consistent with your plan. For example, if you decide to purchase only after examining quarterly profit reports, this rule keeps you from acting rashly based on rumours or excitement. Triggers and guardrails are similar to the lines on a twisting road in that they keep you on course and prevent you from acting out of fright or enthusiasm. By following these guidelines, you maintain control over your actions, resulting in a more disciplined and focused approach to investing.

Building a Foundation of Knowledge and Humility

In the fast-paced world of finance, learning never ends. Markets change, new financial products arise, and global events often alter the environment. Committing to constant learning is one of the most effective techniques to avoid overconfidence and make educated judgements. Staying current on market history, behavioural finance, and economic trends provides insights that allow you to traverse complicated financial environments with clarity and care.

Continuous learning fosters what behavioural economists refer to as "intellectual humility"—the understanding that there is always more to learn. When you view investing as a talent that takes practice and study, you cultivate a mentality that prioritises insight over assumption. This humility balances overconfidence by reminding you that even the finest investors do not have all the answers. For example, examining previous market collapses and bubbles may help you recognise warning indications of unsustainable expansion, even if public opinion is positive.

Commit to reading widely, including books, articles, and reports on anything from stock analysis to economic policy. Attend webinars, join investing clubs, and interact with thought leaders who question traditional beliefs. This technique cultivates a well-rounded viewpoint, allowing you to analyse assets with depth and understanding. Cultivating a lifelong learning mentality enables you to make judgements based on study and analysis rather than intuition or following the herd.

Finding Signal in the Silence

In today's digital era, financial news is constantly updated. We are inundated with information, notifications, and views, producing a feeling of urgency that might impair our judgement. Limiting your exposure to this noise is critical for staying focused on your long-term objectives. Market noise intensifies all price movements, making little swings seem gigantic. However, much of this information is unrelated to your plan, and responding to it might lead to overtrading and rash judgements.

Set limits for your market interaction. Instead of monitoring prices numerous times each day, schedule regular portfolio reviews, such as once a week or after a critical economic report. Use filters on financial platforms to obtain just the most essential updates, emphasising quality over quantity. This method does not include avoiding the market but instead selectively interacting with information that has a meaningful influence on your financial choices.

Limiting your exposure to noise allows you to focus on relevant analysis, which reduces stress and helps you resist the desire to react to every market action. The market is like a river; the currents are constantly shifting, but not every movement necessitates a response. Reducing your exposure helps you remain focused on your objectives, enabling you to make judgements with patience and perspective.

The Power of Patience in Wealth-Building

In an economic world that values immediate victories and riches, patience is a rare and robust virtue. Building money is a marathon, not a sprint, and taking a cautious and steady approach will help you remain robust throughout market fluctuations. Patience helps you to concentrate on long-term progress while avoiding the temptation to respond to every price fluctuation or trend. This approach prioritises longevity above rapid satisfaction, laying the groundwork for a stable future.

A patient attitude allows you to see market changes as usual rather than as triggers for action. It educates you to choose value above price, understanding that genuine wealth-building requires persistence and compounding over time. By refusing the pull of immediate rewards, you may build a portfolio that increases slowly, even if the path is sometimes complicated. This resilience boosts confidence, helping you to manage the market with a feeling of purpose and perspective that lasts beyond the daily grind.

Using patience as a tactic is transformational. It enables you to see through the hoopla and adopt a disciplined, deliberate approach to investing. Patience is the best safeguard against herding and overreaction, reminding you that financial success takes years, not weeks. It is the attitude that prioritises consistency above excitement, leading you to a future of stability, independence, and long-term progress.

It is crucial to create practical procedures that can direct decision-making even in the face of these psychological traps in order to escape herding, overconfidence, and overreaction. First, setting explicit guidelines for decision-making that are focused on individual objectives rather than industry trends is one of the best ways to prevent herding behaviour. Instead of continuously observing market swings, it would be wise to set up predetermined investment triggers, such as automatically selling a stock when it reaches a desired price. This lessens the temptation to follow the herd and keeps you in line with your long-term investing philosophy by eliminating the emotional impulse from the decision-making process.

Reducing overconfidence, which frequently results in bad investment choices, is another essential skill. By consistently challenging your presumptions and avoiding the "confirmation bias" trap, which occurs when we look for evidence that only confirms our preconceptions, you may combat this. Making a commitment to routine portfolio reviews and taking into account input from a variety of sources is a helpful strategy for managing overconfidence. Any blind spots in your analysis can be revealed by hearing from experts who have different opinions and researching topics unrelated to your main area of investment interest. This wider viewpoint prevents overconfidence by promoting more fair assessments.

Applying behavioural economic methods, like commitment devices, can also be very helpful in preventing rash decisions. One way to guarantee that investments are made consistently, irrespective of market conditions, is to set up automatic contributions to an investing plan, such as a dollar-cost averaging (DCA) method. This promotes a long-term view and lessens the emotional burden of each individual choice. By automatically modifying portfolios in accordance with clients' predetermined risk tolerance and long-term objectives, financial institutions like robo-advisors can also include behavioural insights to assist clients in becoming more disciplined investors and reduce decisions motivated by overconfidence or fear.

Additionally, mindfulness is essential for reducing rash decisions. Investors can determine whether their emotional state—whether fear, greed, or excitement—is impacting their decisions by pausing and thinking things through before acting. Making it a habit to write down your choices and consider your feelings amid big market swings is one method to practise mindfulness. By increasing your awareness of how emotions affect your financial decisions and giving you a chance to modify your strategy in real-time, this exercise guarantees more measured reactions to market swings.

Lastly, adopting a methodical approach is essential to investment success. True wealth-building necessitates patience, yet market volatility frequently tempts investors to act quickly in an attempt to achieve short-term gains. This way of thinking entails ignoring the temptation to act on every news item or market movement and accepting market swings as a necessary part of the long-term process. You may let compounding operate in your favour and progressively increase your wealth without succumbing to the psychological traps of overreaction or herd mentality by keeping a patient, long-term perspective.

Investors can cultivate a more disciplined, logical approach to investing by incorporating five strategies: establishing rules and triggers, lowering overconfidence, engaging in mindfulness exercises, committing to learning, and embracing patience. These frameworks encourage long-term wealth-building tactics that can withstand the market's inevitable ups and downs, in addition to steering investors away from rash, emotionally charged decisions.

Chapter 12

The Future of Behavioural Finance: Technology and Investor Biases

As we go farther into the twenty-first century, finance is experiencing a shift that would have been unthinkable only a few decades ago. Technology is altering the laws of investment, influencing how we trade, make choices, and even think about money. Despite these advancements, one thing has remained constant: human psychology. Our biases, inclinations, and emotions are as important to investing now as they were a century ago. What is new today is how technology intensifies these biases, often obscuring the distinction between rational investment and emotional decision-making.

Technology and Behavioural Finance

The intersection of technology and behavioural finance is no longer a theoretical idea; it is there, impacting every click, transaction, and portfolio. In this chapter, we will look at how technology advancements—from artificial intelligence and algorithmic trading to social media and gamified apps—are influencing investor behaviour. We will look at the new biases that these technologies introduce, as well as the tremendous tools they provide to help us become more conscious and potentially in control of our financial choices.

Imagine wandering through a funhouse where every mirror you look at reveals a twisted image of yourself. Financial technology works similarly to mirrors, enhancing certain behaviours while distorting others. With the proliferation of real-time data, social media updates, and algorithmic recommendations, investors are inundated with information and stimulation that exacerbate their inherent biases. Investors used to spend days reading quarterly reports or studying stock charts, but now they are impacted by hourly tweets, news alerts, and market forecasts given directly to their smartphones. Every piece of information, every signal, becomes a potential trigger, driving us to act—sometimes against our better judgement.

Consider the idea of confirmation bias, which refers to our inclination to seek out information that confirms our current opinions while disregarding facts that contradict them. Technology exacerbates this prejudice like never before. If you are optimistic about a stock, computers will tailor your newsfeed to support your optimism, giving you more stories on the company's growth prospects and fewer about its hazards. Investors find themselves in digital echo chambers, seeing just what they want to see, which may lead to hazardous overconfidence. Instead of functioning as a neutral instrument, technology magnifies our strong biases, urging us to make judgements we would not have made otherwise.

Algorithmic trading has transformed the speed and accuracy with which transactions are conducted, enabling financial institutions to make split-second choices that take advantage of slight price swings. However, this power has a psychological cost for individual investors, who may feel carried away by a market that moves too quickly for them to fathom. For ordinary investors, the speed set by algorithms gives them a sense of control—if they could move as rapidly, they, too, might benefit. This mindset may rise to action bias—the desire to do whatever to remain in the game.

Apps that provide real-time trading alternatives are hazardous since they encourage users to approach the stock market like a video game. Users may purchase or sell stocks in an instant by pressing a button, frequently based on little more than a gut sensation or a fleeting trend. This access, although empowering, might jeopardise disciplined, long-term investment. By focusing on short-term swings rather than long-term development, investors are vulnerable to a variety of biases, ranging from herding to overtrading. Algorithmic trading, which is built for speed, fosters a mindset that encourages impulsivity, enticing investors to hurry rather than prudently.

In an age when social media has an impact on everything from politics to lifestyle choices, it is no wonder that investing has been drawn into its circle. Twitter, Reddit, and even Instagram have become hubs for financial advice, stock recommendations, and speculative analysis. What is the problem? Social media is essentially social, designed to increase popularity rather than truth. When investors assemble in these virtual places, they create an echo chamber in which opinions are reinforced rather than challenged, resulting in phenomena such as herding bias.

Consider the spectacular emergence of "meme stocks," in which firms with weak fundamentals find their shares skyrocket solely because they have piqued the interest of an online community. This tendency demonstrates the sheer strength of collective sentiment—as well as its limitations. When a large number of individuals believe in a stock's potential, their combined activities may push up prices, resulting in a self-fulfilling prophecy that finally spirals out of control. Social media exacerbates this impact by increasing the speed with which individuals may influence one another and act on collective thoughts, frequently with little concern for fundamental analysis. For many, this climate generates an "us versus them" mindset, pitting regular investors against institutional actors and exacerbating irrational decision-making and groupthink.

Artificial Intelligence and Finance

AI promises a future in which investors are more knowledgeable, efficient, and aware of market trends. However, as AI infiltrates every part of our financial life, it has the potential to accentuate our prejudices, quietly impacting our judgements in ways we may not fully comprehend. In this chapter, we will look at how artificial intelligence (AI) and other developing technologies are redefining behavioural finance, transforming not just the market but also our attitude to life and investment.

One of the most transformational ways AI is affecting banking is via data—its capacity to collect, analyse, and understand vast amounts of information at rates that no human could ever equal. This real-time analysis is transforming how we make choices, giving insights that can detect anything from macroeconomic movements to micro-level stock performance within seconds. AI provides investors with new tools for analysing financial data, evaluating business health, tracking global economic indicators, and even monitoring social media sentiment to forecast stock moves.

However, although this quantity of data is valid, it also presents issues. The sheer number of information provided by artificial intelligence may overwhelm investors, resulting in what psychologists refer to as information overload. When confronted with an overwhelming amount of data, we may resort to mental shortcuts, selecting the information that is most readily available or familiar—a cognitive bias known as the availability heuristic. With AI providing us with a continual stream of data, there is a risk that we may become more reactive, making judgements based on what is instantly available rather than what is strategically sensible.

Furthermore, AI-powered systems may prioritise current data over past patterns, leading investors to concentrate on short-term swings rather than long-term development. Consider an AI system that detects stocks based on daily social media sentiment like a tool that might cause investors to overestimate the importance of short-term public opinion, exacerbating biases like herding and overreaction. As a consequence, although AI provides tools for making better-informed judgements, it also requires investors to learn new skills, such as critically evaluating the relevance and usefulness of data and resisting the impulse to act on the latest trend.

With AI's advanced prediction algorithms, investors might easily fall into the trap of thinking the market is more predictable than it really is. AI's capabilities are really astounding—it can analyse previous data, discover trends, and make projections with remarkable precision. However, markets are impacted by a wide range of circumstances, including political upheavals and natural calamities, which no computer can anticipate with precision. The risk here is overconfidence, the notion that since we have superior instruments at our disposal, we can outperform the market.

This illusion of predictability is a significant area where AI might deceive humans. For example, AI may detect a continuous trend in a sector based on many years of data, leading investors to see it as a "safe bet." However, unanticipated occurrences, such as the 2020 pandemic, might upset even the most stable patterns. When investors depend too much on AI estimates, they may acquire a feeling of invincibility, believing that the past always predicts the future. This overconfidence may result in increased risk-taking and, eventually, increased exposure to possible losses.

To counteract this, investors must remember that AI is a tool, not a crystal ball. AI's predictive capacity is best utilised as a guide, allowing investors to assess possibilities rather than certainties. Critical thinking and care remain needed since relying too much on AI's "predictions" might expose investors to dangers they do not fully grasp. Embracing AI insights is beneficial, but combining them with a healthy appreciation for market volatility is critical for long-term success.

Robo-advisors have democratised investing advice, allowing millions of people to access financial planning that was previously too sophisticated or out of reach. These AI-powered systems provide automated investing plans, portfolio management, and even tax optimisation, all at a fraction of the cost of conventional consultants. By completing a few questions, investors may obtain a personalised portfolio based on their risk tolerance, financial objectives, and timetable, with modifications made automatically as circumstances change.

However, as easy as robo-advisors are, they might lead to automation bias, which is the inclination to believe computerised solutions without evaluating their validity. Investors may think that an AI suggestion must be optimum, decreasing their involvement in the decision-making process. This passive dependence might result in a limited comprehension of one's portfolio and financial objectives. In the long run, investors may need more expertise and insight to react if market conditions or personal circumstances change in ways that the robo-advisor was not designed to manage.

Robo-advisers also need to gain the personal touch that human advisors provide. They cannot discern subtle emotional signals, life events, or personal preferences that may impact an investor's requirements. While robo-advisors provide a helpful entrance point, they should be seen as beginning points for financial planning rather than alternatives for personal interaction. For investors, the future rests in finding a balance—using AI technologies to guide their strategy while also taking a hands-on approach to understanding and adapting their financial path as life changes.

Social Media and Finance

Social media has generated an unprecedented phenomenon: investing groups acting in concert, fuelled by viral postings, "likes," and collective enthusiasm. Platforms such as Twitter and Reddit have become battlegrounds where ideas circulate quickly, resulting in waves of herding behaviour. These online platforms reinforce social proof, a bias in which individuals believe that if others are investing in something, it must be a good decision. Despite poor fundamentals, stocks such as GameStop and AMC rose to prominence as a result of Redditors' support.

The consequences of this digital herding are significant. Investors are subjected to a powerful combination of groupthink and short-term rewards, which often drown out basic research and logical judgement. Social media drives investors to move swiftly for fear of missing out on the next great thing. This herd mentality is fuelled by AI algorithms that watch trends and rapidly identify "hot stocks," giving followers a false feeling of security that they are making the right choice.

To break away from the allure of social media, investors must develop discipline and filter out the noise. AI-powered platforms might assist by recognising dangerous behaviours and urging consumers to think before making rash transactions based on viral information. The difficulty is to strike a balance between the feeling of community and shared insights that social media offers and a commitment to independent, evidence-based decision-making. In the future, AI might play a role in regulating these areas, warning users about the hazards of mob mentality and assisting them in making decisions based on individual objectives rather than collective inclinations.

Despite these issues, AI has the potential to function as an accountability partner, assisting investors in recognising and mitigating their biases. AI can detect overtrading, excessive risk-taking, and confirmation bias by analysing trends in user behaviour. Consider getting a signal that shows how often you have traded impulsively in reaction to market declines or a warning that you are focussing too much on current performance data rather than historical patterns.

Bias detection is a game-changing invention since it allows investors to see a reflection of their behaviour, increasing self-awareness and leading to improved decision-making. AI-powered platforms may soon provide personalised coaching, assisting users in setting precise objectives for bias management. For example, an investor who is prone to overreaction may get frequent reminders to assess their long-term plan before making short-term transactions, promoting attention and discipline.

AI may also help investors adopt behaviours that encourage logical thinking. For example, several platforms are experimenting with "cooling-off" features that restrict trading during volatile times, assisting the customers to avoid making rash decisions. By serving as a virtual coach, AI has the potential to encourage a more deliberate, less impulsive approach to investing, assisting investors in developing habits that promote long-term growth and stability.

The most promising aspect of AI in banking is its capacity to provide completely personalised experiences. With AI, financial planning may go beyond essential counsel, adapting suggestions to each person's specific financial status, lifestyle, and aspirations. Imagine a platform that learns not just your financial history but also your personality, beliefs, and emotional triggers, resulting in a strategy that represents who you are rather than simply what you earn or owe.

For example, if AI determines that you are particularly risk-averse, it may offer a more conservative portfolio or tools to boost your confidence in riskier assets. It might include particular recommendations for dealing with anxiety during market downturns, as well as materials that explain complicated financial topics in ways that are appropriate for your learning style. This kind of personalisation has the potential to redefine the way individuals interact with their money, shifting investing from a one-size-fits-all paradigm to a profoundly personalised path that grows with each individual.

As AI advances, it may even assist investors in overcoming subconscious prejudices by developing methods that take into account human preferences and psychological triggers. The future is more than simply making better trades; it is also about employing technology to promote financial well-being. AI might transform the way we think about money, turning it into a tool for self-discovery, empowerment, and progress.

Technology is influencing behavioural finance in previously unthinkable ways as it develops further. The impact of artificial intelligence on investor behaviour is among the most significant advancements. AI makes it possible to process enormous volumes of data at previously unheard-of rates, giving individual investors access to insights that were previously unattainable. AI tools like ChatGPT and algorithmic trading systems are revolutionising the way investors make decisions by providing real-time analysis of macroeconomic data, global market movements, and even sentiment from social media. These technologies can have drawbacks, too, as they may unintentionally reinforce preexisting biases. An emphasis on immediate market fluctuations, for example, could result from using AI to analyse patterns based on short-term data. This could cause overreaction and encourage impulsive trading decisions. Investors may get overconfident and disregard the underlying complexity and unpredictability of markets, thinking that AI's predictions are infallible.

By speeding up information flow, 5G technology exacerbates these issues even more, raising market volatility and even evoking stronger emotional reactions among investors. Faster information dissemination increases the urge to respond quickly, which might result in impulsive behaviour motivated by FOMO. As investors hurry to respond to the newest information without thoroughly weighing the long-term effects of their choices, this quick spread of news and updates can heighten the emotional tone of market activity and increase herd behaviour. Because 5G speeds up communication and makes market data more accessible, it fosters a culture that rewards reactionary behaviour, which raises the possibility of overreaction and herd mentality. Because they have to sort through the deluge of information and market signals, investors are forced to face their prejudices more often.

Other Technologies and Future

Furthermore, by adding a new degree of transparency and autonomy, blockchain technology and decentralised finance (DeFi) are changing the financial environment. These technologies create additional complications even while they have the potential to lessen biases, such as by removing information asymmetry in financial markets. Although blockchain's decentralised structure makes it possible to be more independent from conventional financial institutions, it also raises the possibility of speculative activity and the emergence of new bubbles. Investors may succumb to the same biases that have existed in traditional markets, such as herd mentality or overconfidence, in DeFi platforms. As we've seen with previous market bubbles, the allure of large profits combined with inadequate regulation and control can result in the development of speculative settings where irrational exuberance takes root.

In terms of the wider ramifications, blockchain and artificial intelligence are altering the function of financial institutions, presenting investors with both opportunities and hazards. By providing individualised investment recommendations at a fraction of the price of traditional financial consultants, robo-advisors—powered by artificial intelligence—are already democratising access to financial advice. But automation bias, in which investors mindlessly accept algorithmic recommendations without fully comprehending the underlying assumptions or risks, could result from these AI-driven platforms. These platforms facilitate investing, but they also promote passive reliance on technology, which may keep people from actively participating in their financial choices.

Furthermore, investors may overestimate the accuracy of these forecasts due to AI's capacity to forecast market moves by examining historical patterns. No matter how advanced, AI models are prone to mistakes in volatile conditions because they cannot take into account all the factors that affect market dynamics, such as natural disasters or political unrest. An over-reliance on AI forecasts may give investors a false sense of control and predictability, which could encourage them to take on more risk because they think AI has made the market more predictable than it actually is.

Whereas blockchain, 5G, and AI provide significant advantages in terms of accessibility and market efficiency, they also add new levels of complexity to investor behaviour. By making information more rapid and accessible, these technologies increase biases and may cause people to make more emotional decisions. Investors must approach AI with caution and critical thinking as it continues to transform the financial industry, understanding that it has the ability to both positively and negatively impact their decision-making. How well investors can adjust to these technological developments while controlling the biases that technology itself may exacerbate will determine the direction of behavioural finance in the future.

The ability of technology and human judgement to collaborate is crucial for the future of behavioural finance. We must strike a balance between the insights provided by AI and machine learning and our natural grasp of market psychology as we become more dependent on these technologies. AI's function is to enhance human intuition rather than replace it, giving investors a more comprehensive understanding of potential risks and rewards. AI, for instance, can spot trends or irregularities in data that people might overlook, while humans can use their emotional intelligence and contextual knowledge to understand the results. In this way, human input combined with technology can produce a more robust decision-making process that takes into consideration both emotional intelligence and reason.

Additionally, the developments in AI might help investors identify and address their biases. Technology can be used as a tool for self-awareness and accountability rather than to reinforce human faults. Investors can more effectively combine AI-driven insights with a methodical, long-term investment plan as they grow more conscious of the ways in which biases like confirmation bias, loss aversion, and overconfidence affect their choices. Technology serves as a guide and a check in this mutually beneficial connection, offering insights while also assisting in reducing the very biases that could impair informed judgement. We may, therefore, envision a future in which technical improvements and human intellect combine to produce more intelligent, well-rounded investing plans by seeing technology as an ally in enhancing decision-making rather than as a force that reduces human agency.

Conclusion

As we near the finish of our voyage, we see that the tale of finance is not just about stocks, charts, or economic cycles; it is about us. It is about the human experience, our natural desires, blind spots, and the unwavering desire to build our destiny. This book delves into the secret depths of behavioural finance, uncovering the factors that shape our financial life and providing us with a fresh perspective on the market and ourselves.

During our investigation, we experienced the grand draw of herding, the temptation of overconfidence, and the trap of overreaction. We have seen that these biases are more than simply oddities of human nature; they are the currents that drive market movements and, in some cases, whole economies. Understanding these dynamics allows us to navigate the financial world with a more transparent lens, seeing the pressures that often sway us off course. However, awareness is just the beginning.

In this book, we have progressed beyond detecting biases to conquering them, turning knowledge into action and insight into strategy. You now have the skills to develop your investing philosophy, stop and think when emotions are strong, and make decisions that are consistent with your beliefs and long-term objectives. These tools will allow you to break away from the mob, invest independently, and approach every financial choice with clarity and purpose.

In the future, technology will play a significant role in the financial landscape. Artificial intelligence, algorithmic trading, and social media-driven markets are altering finance in ways we are just starting to understand. AI opens to us previously unheard-of opportunities for data analysis and predictive insights, but it also magnifies the biases we have discovered in ways that must be avoided. In this era of quick updates, digital trends, and real-time decisions, the most successful investors will not only have the most significant algorithms, but they will also understand how to utilise these tools without allowing them to dictate their choices.

Consider a world in which you are not simply another investor, responding to every spike and decline, but a controller of your financial destiny. With the knowledge and tactics in this book, you can become that investor. You can weather the market's inevitable ups and downs with tenacity, investing not merely for profit but also for a cause that matches your innermost beliefs and goals. In an era of data and digital speed, your most significant advantage is your understanding—of markets, technology, and, most crucially, yourself.

So, once you finish this book, realise that the journey continues. The field of behavioural finance provides lifetime lessons that will develop as markets change and new technologies arise. Each investment, each decision, and each market moment is an opportunity to apply these lessons, fine-tune your strategy, and invest with ever-greater insight and confidence.

Thank you for joining me on this journey via behavioural finance. May the thoughts in these pages encourage you to see money as a path of self-discovery, freedom, and purpose. Here is to a future in which you invest not just with wisdom but also with purpose, perceiving the market—and yourself—with fresh clarity and power.

References

Baker, H. K., Filbeck, G., & Nofsinger, J. R. (2019). *Behavioural finance: what everyone needs to know®*. Oxford University Press. https://doi.org/10.1093/wentk/9780190868741.001.0001

Baker, M., & Wurgler, J. (2006). Investor Sentiment and the Cross-Section of Stock Returns. *Journal of Finance* 61, no. 4, 1645-1680. https://doi.org/10.1111/j.1540-6261.2006.00885.x

Banerjee, A. V. (1992). A Simple Model of Herd Behaviour. *Quarterly Journal of Economics* 107, no. 3, 797-817. https://doi.org/10.2307/2118364

Barber, B. M., & Odean, T. (2000). Trading Is Hazardous to Your Wealth: The Common Stock Investment Performance of Individual Investors. *Journal of Finance* 55, no. 2, 773-806. https://doi.org/10.1111/0022-1082.00226

Bikhchandani, S., Hirshleifer, D. & Welch, I. (1992). A Theory of Fads, Fashion, Custom, and Cultural Change as Informational Cascades. *Journal of Political Economy* 100, no. 5, 992-1026. https://doi.org/10.1086/261849

De Bondt, W. F., & Thaler, R. (1985). Does the stock market overreact? *The Journal of finance*, 40(3), 793-805. https://doi.org/10.1111/j.1540-6261.1985.tb05004.x

Fama, E. F. (1970). Efficient Capital Markets: A Review of Theory and Empirical Work. *Journal of Finance* 25, no. 2, 383-417. https://doi.org/10.2307/2325486

Gans Combe, C., Kim, J. Y., Mouhali, W., & Baccar, A. (2023). Making green growth a reality: Coordinating sobriety with stakeholder satisfaction. *PLOS ONE*, 18(8), e0284487. https://doi.org/10.1371/journal.pone.0284487

Gigerenzer, G. (2015). *Simply rational: Decision making in the real world*. Oxford University Press, USA. https://doi.org/10.1093/acprof:oso/9780199390076.001.0001

Kahneman, D., & Tversky, A. (1979). Prospect Theory: An Analysis of Decision under Risk. *Econometrica* 47, no. 2, 263-291. https://doi.org/10.2307/1914185

Kahneman, D., & Tversky, A. (2013). Prospect theory: An analysis of decision under risk. In *Handbook of the fundamentals of financial decision making: Part I* (pp. 99-127). https://doi.org/10.1142/9789814417358_0006

Keynes, J. M. (1936). *The General Theory of Employment Interest and Money*. Macmillan and Company.

Lavoie, M. (2014). Post-Keynesian economics: new foundations. In *Post-Keynesian Economics*. Edward Elgar Publishing. https://doi.org/10.4337/9781783475827.00006

Markowitz, H. M. (1952). Portfolio selection. *The Journal of Finance, 7*(1), 77-91. https://doi.org/10.1111/j.1540-6261.1952.tb01525.x

Odean, T. (1998). Are Investors Reluctant to Realize Their Losses? *Journal of Finance* 53, no. 5, 1775-1798. https://doi.org/10.1111/0022-1082.00072

Petri, F. (2021). *Microeconomics for the critical mind: mainstream and heterodox analyses* (Vol. 1). Cham: Springer. https://doi.org/10.1007/978-3-030-62070-7

Richards, C. (2024). *The behaviour gap: Simple ways to stop doing dumb things with money*. Penguin Group.

Shaikh, A. (2010). Reflexivity, path dependence, and disequilibrium dynamics. *Journal of Post Keynesian Economics, 33*(1), 3-16. https://doi.org/10.2753/PK E0160-3477330101

Shefrin, H. & Statman, M. (1985). The Disposition to Sell Winners Too Early and Ride Losers Too Long: Theory and Evidence. *Journal of Finance* 40, no. 3, 777-790. https://doi.org/10.1111/j.1540-6261.1985.tb05002.x

Shiller, R. J. (2000). *Irrational Exuberance*. Princeton University Press.

Sraffa, P. (1961). Production of commodities by means of commodities. *Science and Society, 25*(2).

Thaler, R. H. (2015). *Misbehaving: The Making of Behavioural Economics*. New York: W.W. Norton & Company.

Index

A

artificial intelligence, xvi, xviii, xix, 37, 135, 137, 140, 141

B

Behavioural Finance, xiii, xv, 2, 17
Bitcoin, xviii, 3, 4, 7, 43, 51, 82, 109
bubble, xv, xviii, 5, 8, 12, 15, 18, 36, 37, 38, 39, 40, 43, 47, 49, 50, 51, 61, 62, 63, 77, 83, 105, 109, 117, 118

C

CAPM, vii, 14, 17, 18, 19, 22
crises, xv, 18, 22, 25, 26, 43, 99

E

Efficient Market Hypothesis, vii, xiii, 2, 8, 17, 19
EMH, vii, 8, 12, 13, 14, 18, 20, 26
emotions, xiii, xiv, 1, 2, 3, 6, 7, 8, 9, 11, 13, 15, 16, 17, 18, 20, 27, 32, 49, 75, 76, 83, 84, 85, 88, 89, 96, 97, 99, 102, 112, 124, 125, 128, 129, 132, 143

F

fear of missing out, 3, 31, 37, 40, 49, 104, 129, 139
FOMO, vii, 3, 8, 31, 37, 49, 51, 52, 104, 122, 129, 141

H

herding, ix, xiii, xiv, xv, xvii, 3, 4, 7, 17, 19, 23, 25, 26, 29, 30, 31, 32, 33, 34, 35, 37, 38, 39, 40, 41, 42, 43, 46, 47, 48, 49, 50, 51, 52, 53, 54, 109, 110, 112, 129, 131, 136, 137, 139, 143

I

irrational behaviour, xv, xviii, 7, 8, 13, 16, 18, 103, 125

L

loss aversion, xiii, 6, 8, 13, 15, 16, 19, 83, 90, 105, 106, 111, 125, 142

M

Market anomalies, 75, 76
MPT, vii, 14, 17, 19

N

NASDAQ, vii, 36

O

Overconfidence, xiv, xv, xvii, 2, 4, 5, 7, 15, 20, 56, 59, 61, 62, 63, 66, 67, 68, 78, 101, 104, 106
overreaction, ix, xiv, xv, xvii, 2, 6, 19, 48, 73, 74, 75, 77, 78, 79, 83, 84, 85, 86, 87, 88, 89, 90, 91, 95, 96, 97, 98, 99, 100, 130, 131, 133, 137, 139, 140, 141, 143

P

Prospect Theory, 15, 17, 19, 21, 26, 83, 145
psychology, xiii, xv, xvi, xvii, xix, xx, 9, 11, 13, 19, 34, 36, 42, 43, 54, 74, 75, 76, 77, 80, 82, 83, 85, 86, 88, 96, 102, 111, 125, 142

S

Social media, xviii, 124, 136, 139
stock market, 3, 17, 20, 22, 23, 24, 25, 42, 58, 79, 80, 81, 97, 103, 111, 119, 136, 145

T

tulip mania, xiii

V

volatility, xiv, 6, 7, 17, 22, 37, 39, 43, 47, 49, 59, 66, 68, 74, 79, 82, 83, 84, 85, 96, 97, 98, 103, 105, 125, 126, 129, 132, 138, 141

www.ingramcontent.com/pod-product-compliance
Lightning Source LLC
Chambersburg PA
CBHW052013230326
41598CB00078B/3329